Turtle Coloring Book

For adults and animal lovers

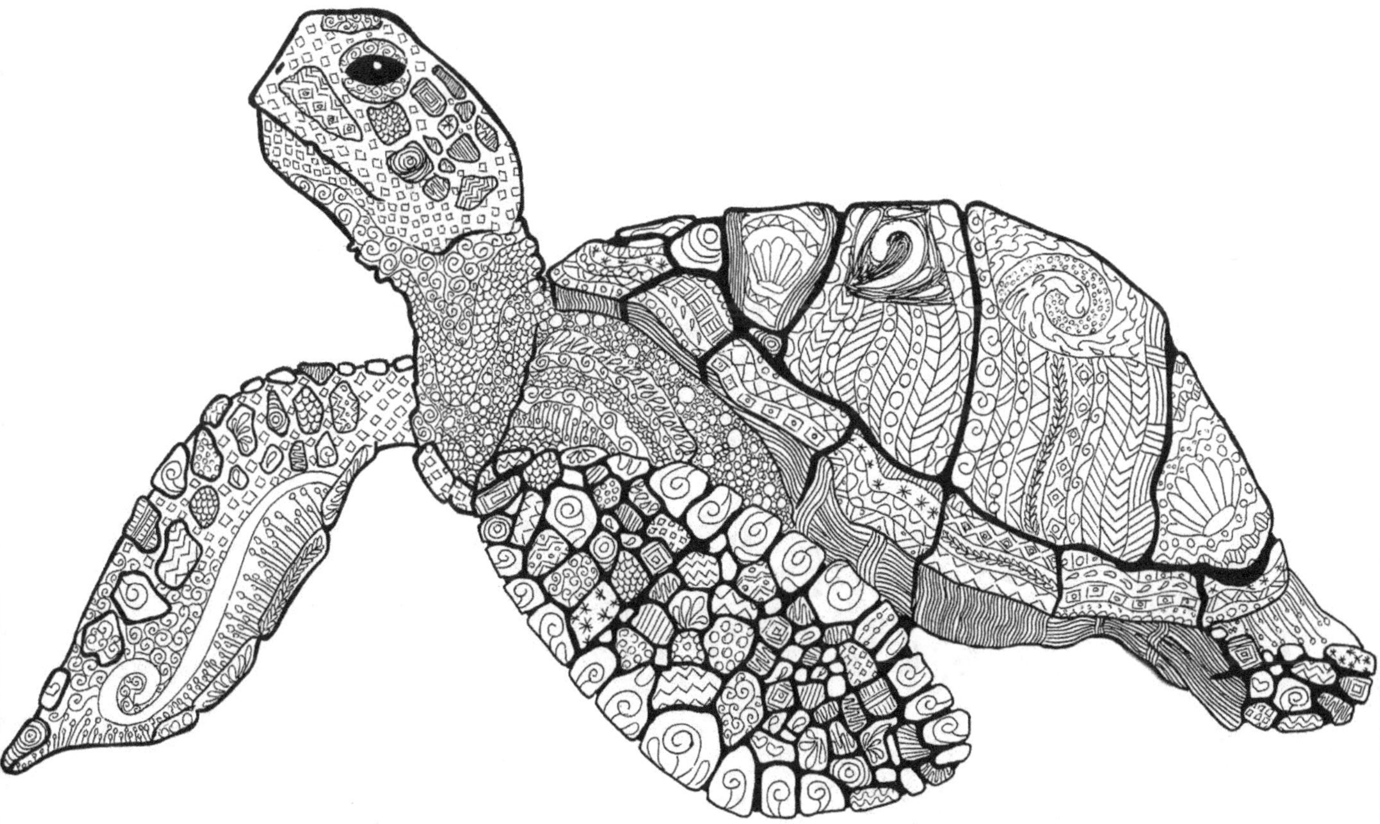

Preview Pages

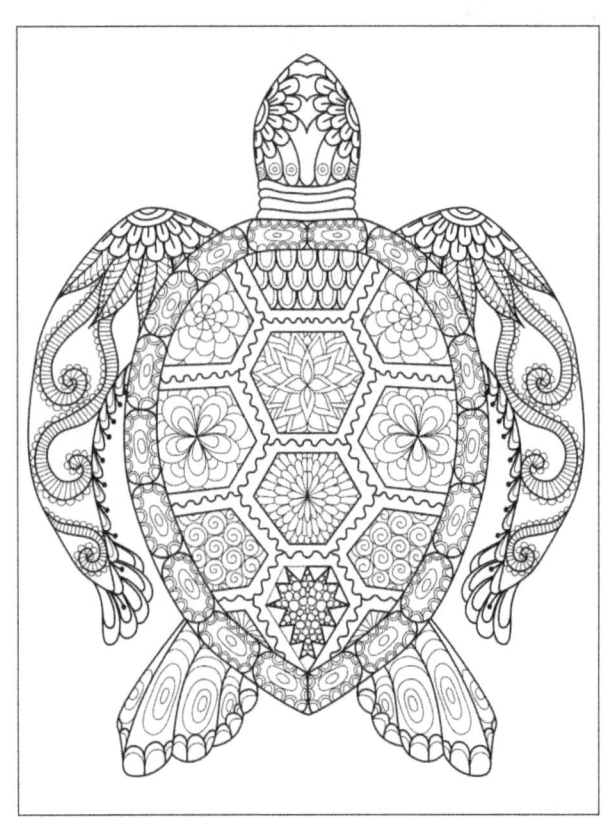
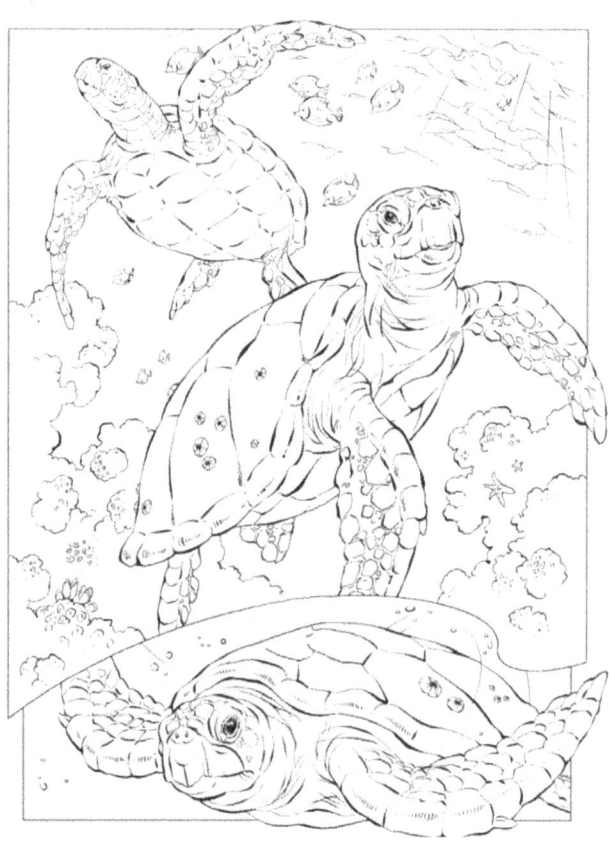
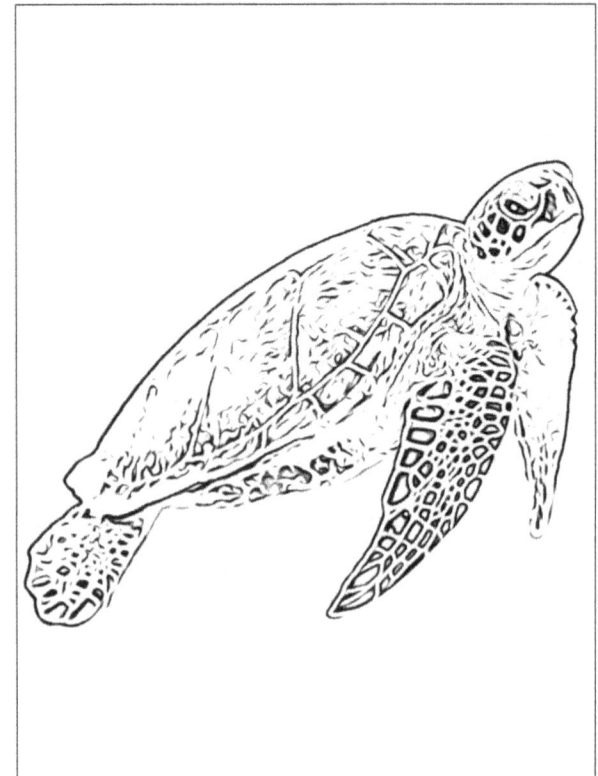
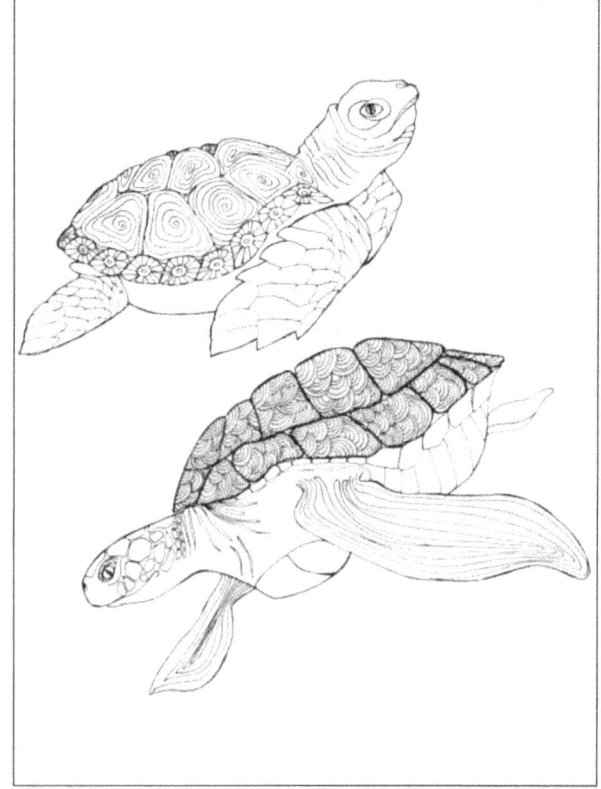

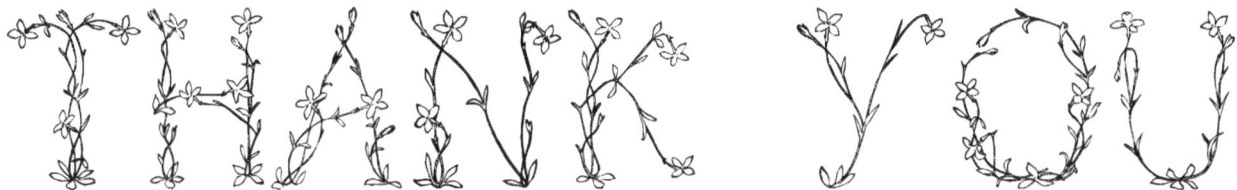

for taking the time out of your busy day to bring life to the images in this book with your colorful imagination!

We hope they bring you a lot of joy and help with stress relief and relaxation.

Inside these pages you'll find simple, complex and realistic designs as well as some cool abstract images to really let your creativity go wild!

To show our appreciation, we've included 5 bonus images in this book that may hint at future publications...look out for them.

Have fun and be kind to animals!

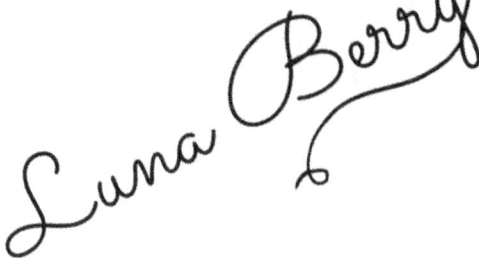

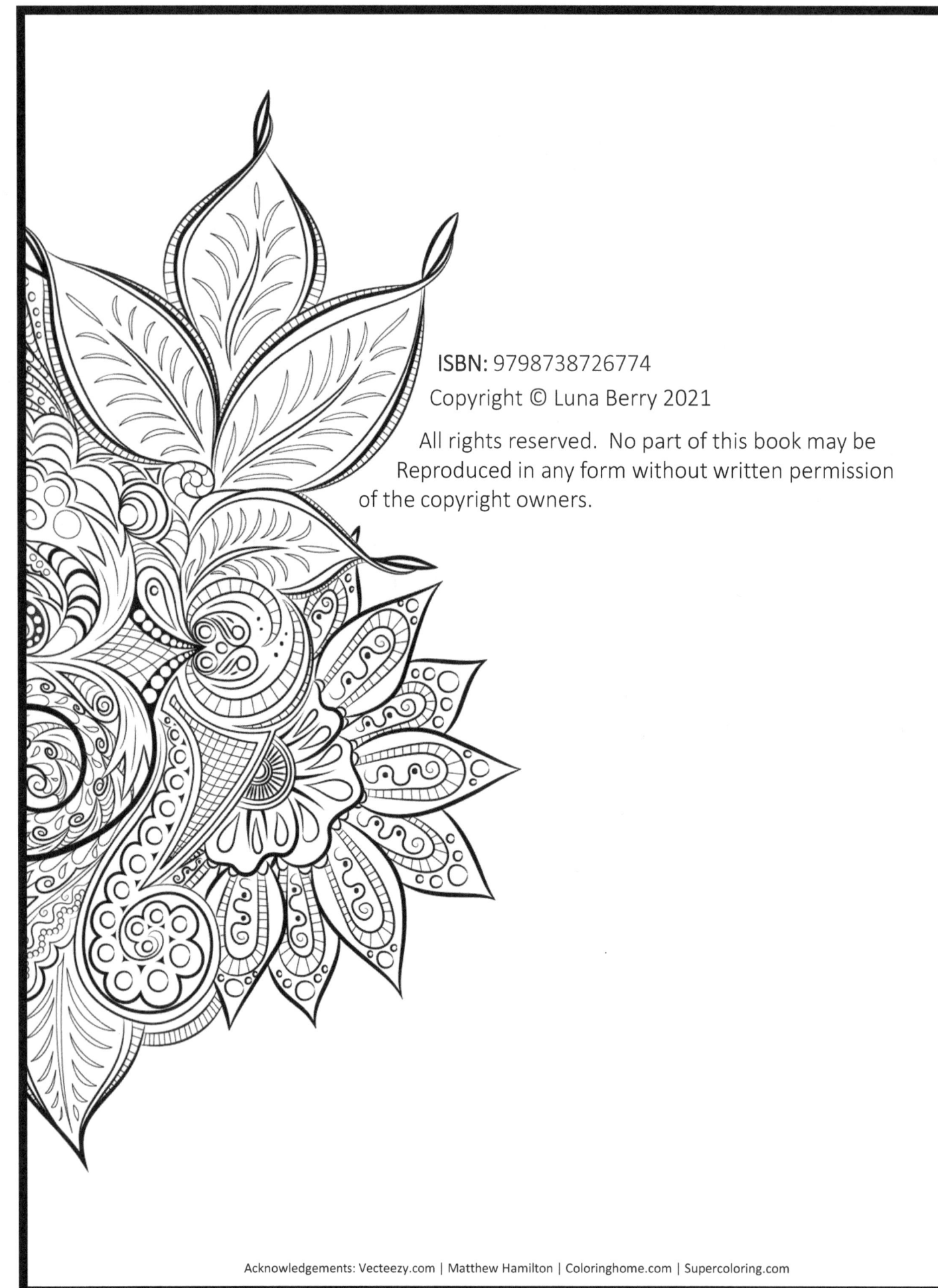

ISBN: 9798738726774

Copyright © Luna Berry 2021

All rights reserved. No part of this book may be Reproduced in any form without written permission of the copyright owners.

Acknowledgements: Vecteezy.com | Matthew Hamilton | Coloringhome.com | Supercoloring.com

COLOR TEST PAGE

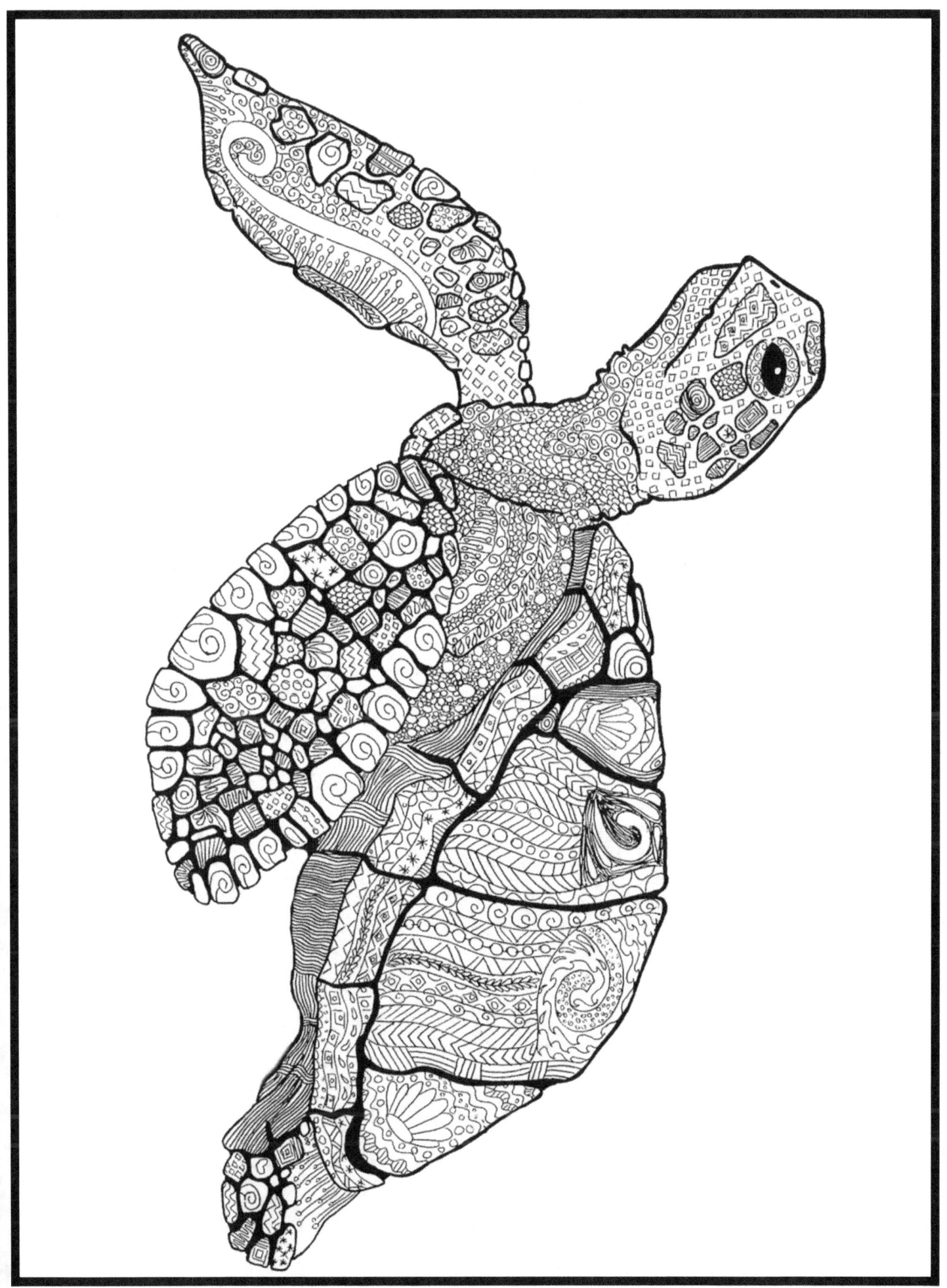

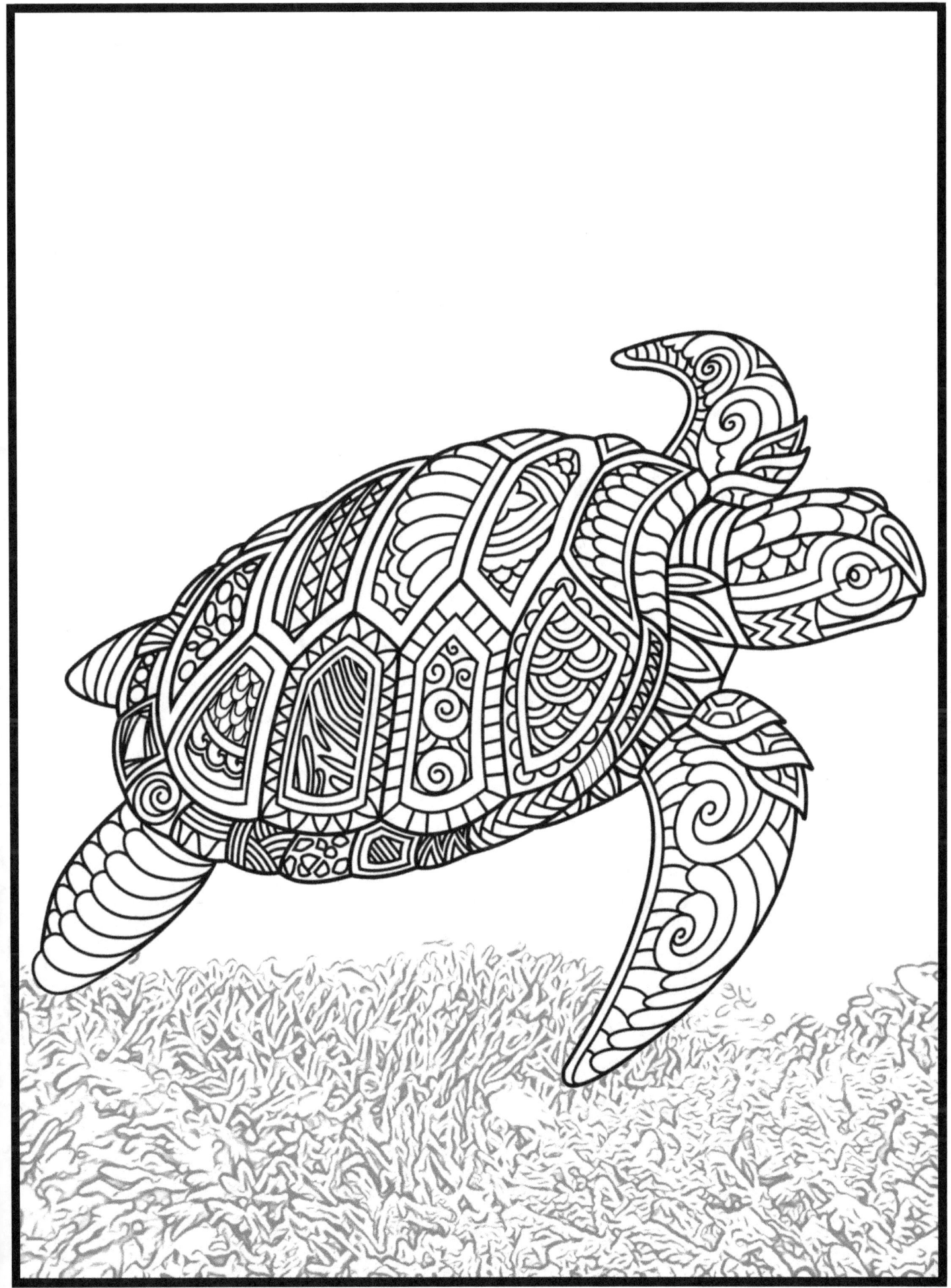

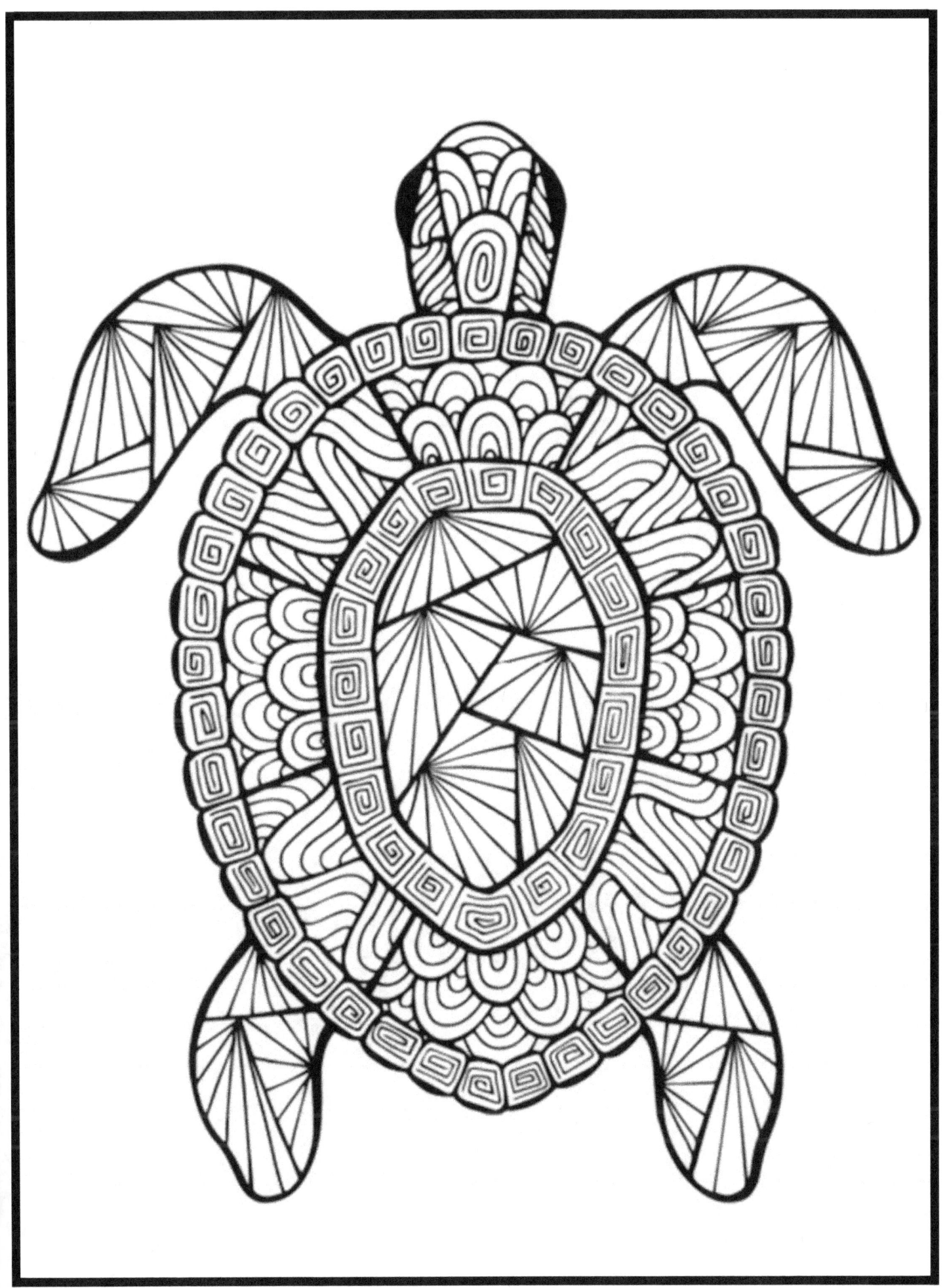

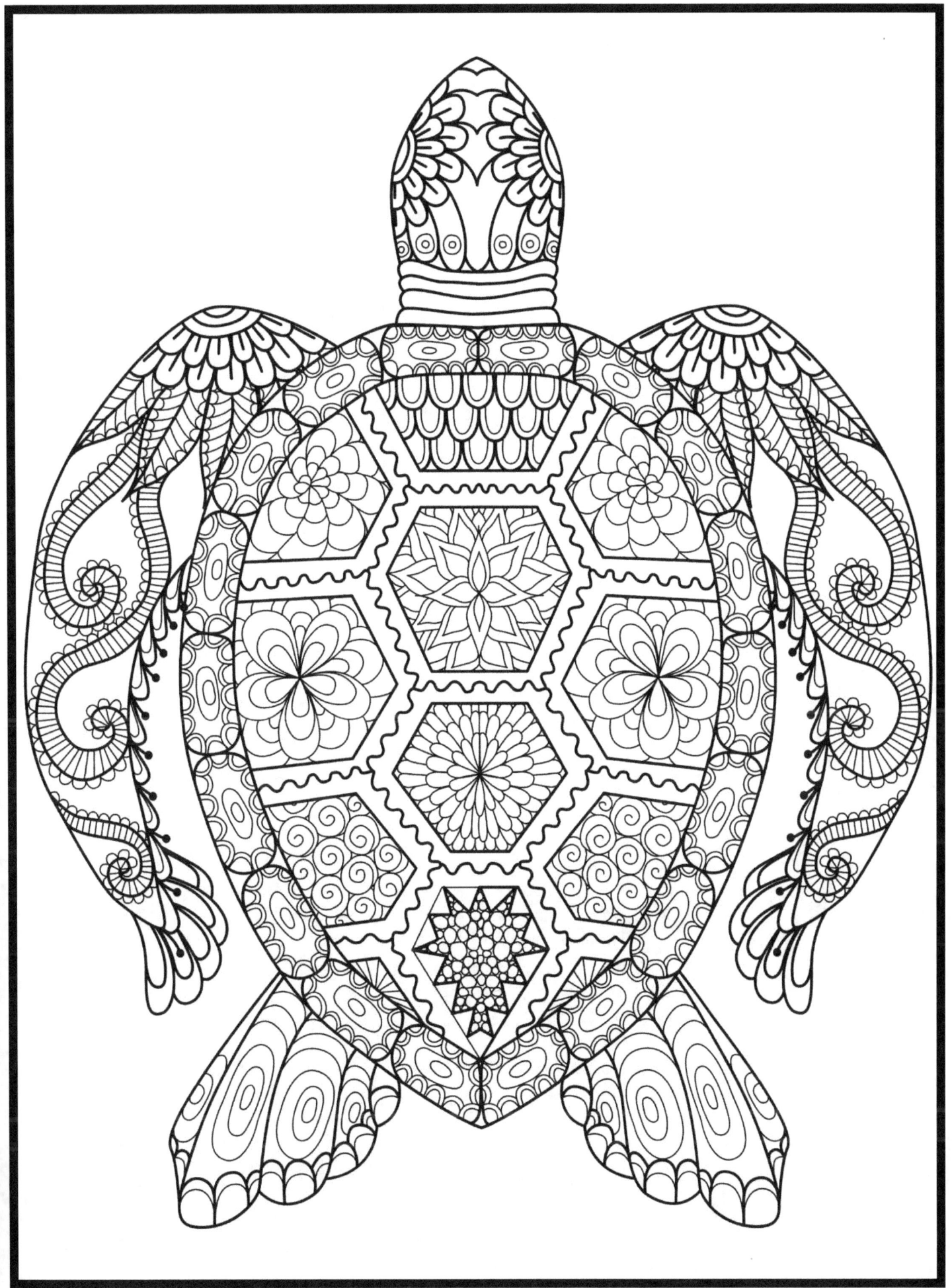

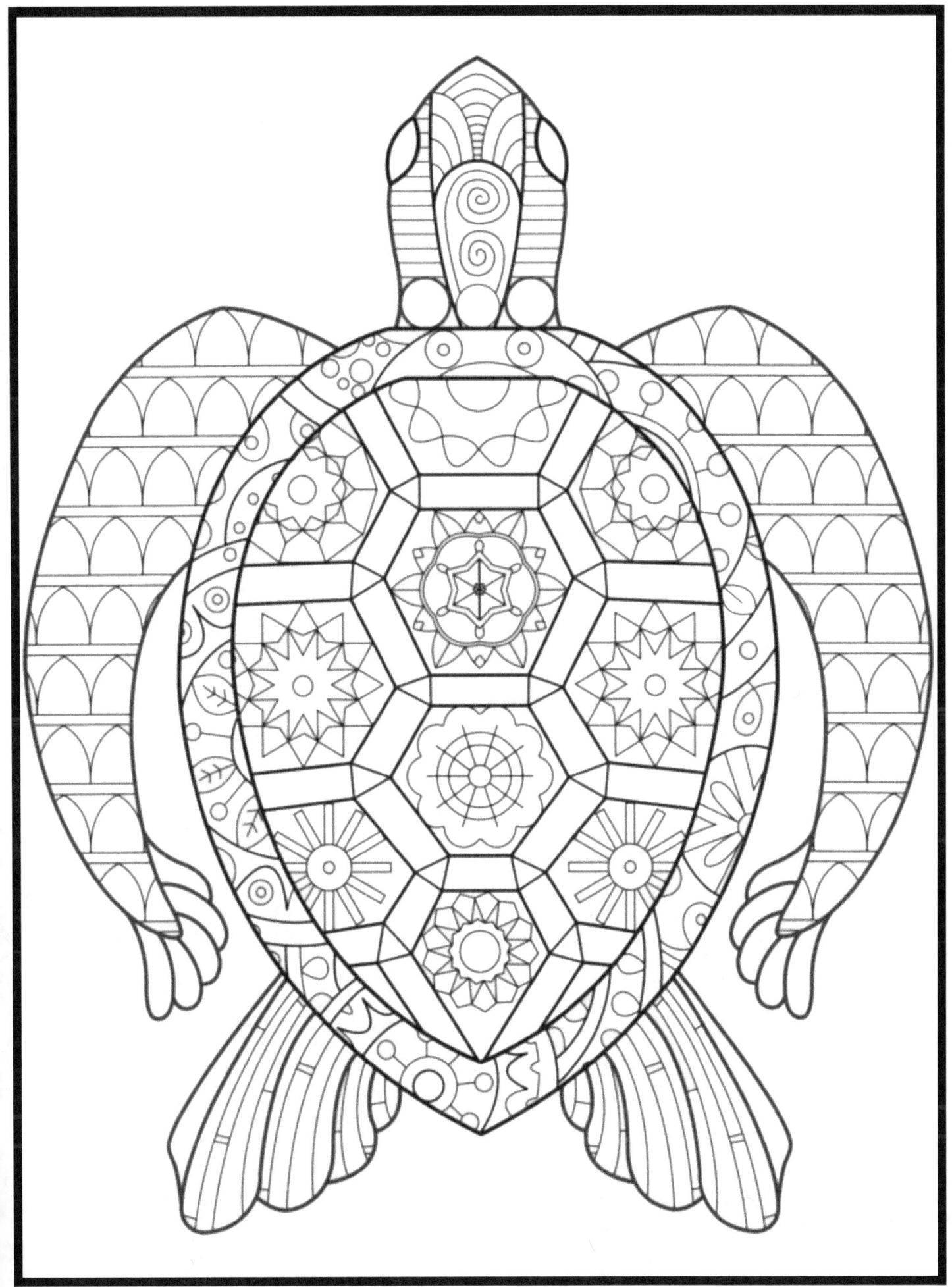

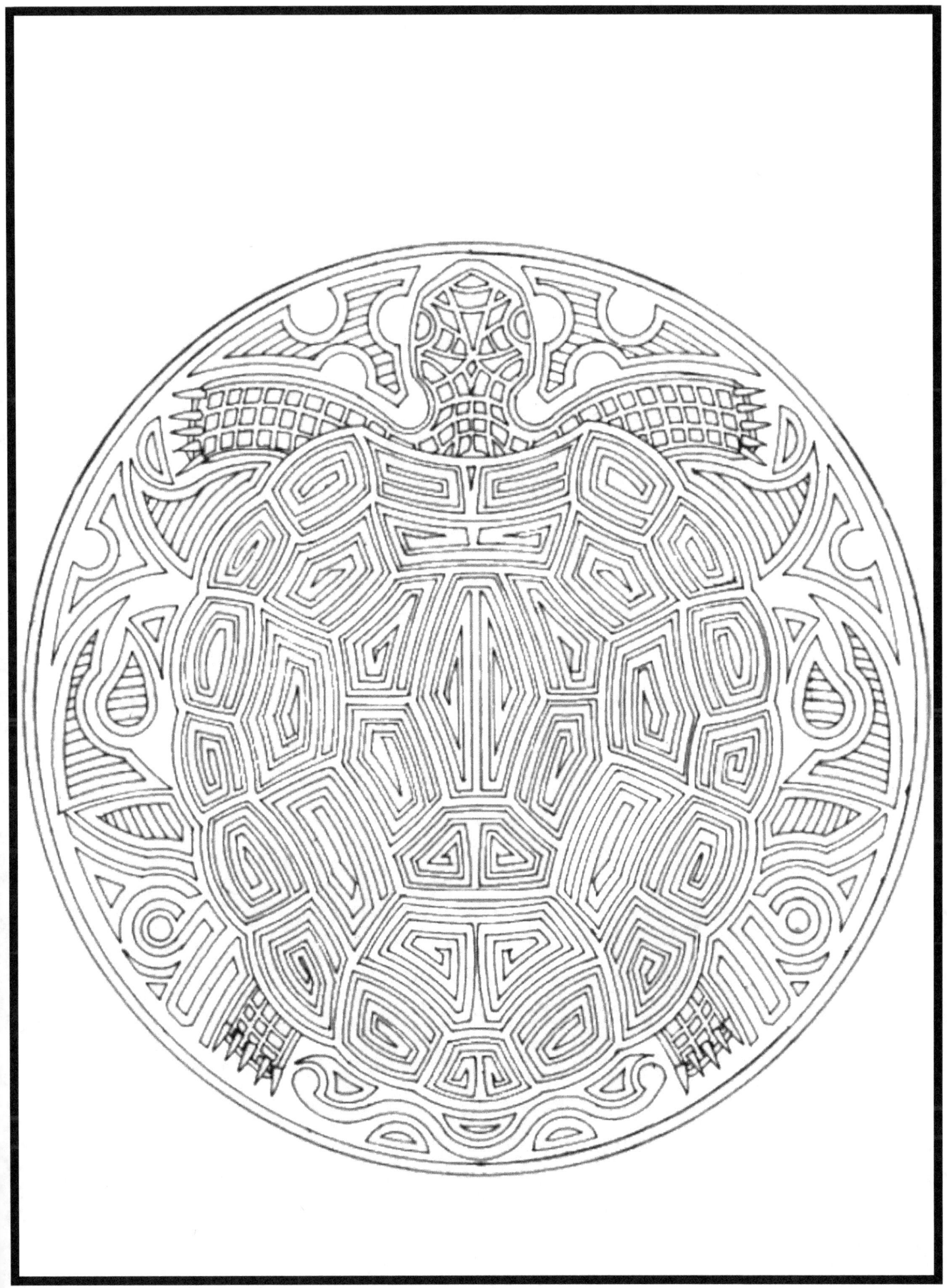

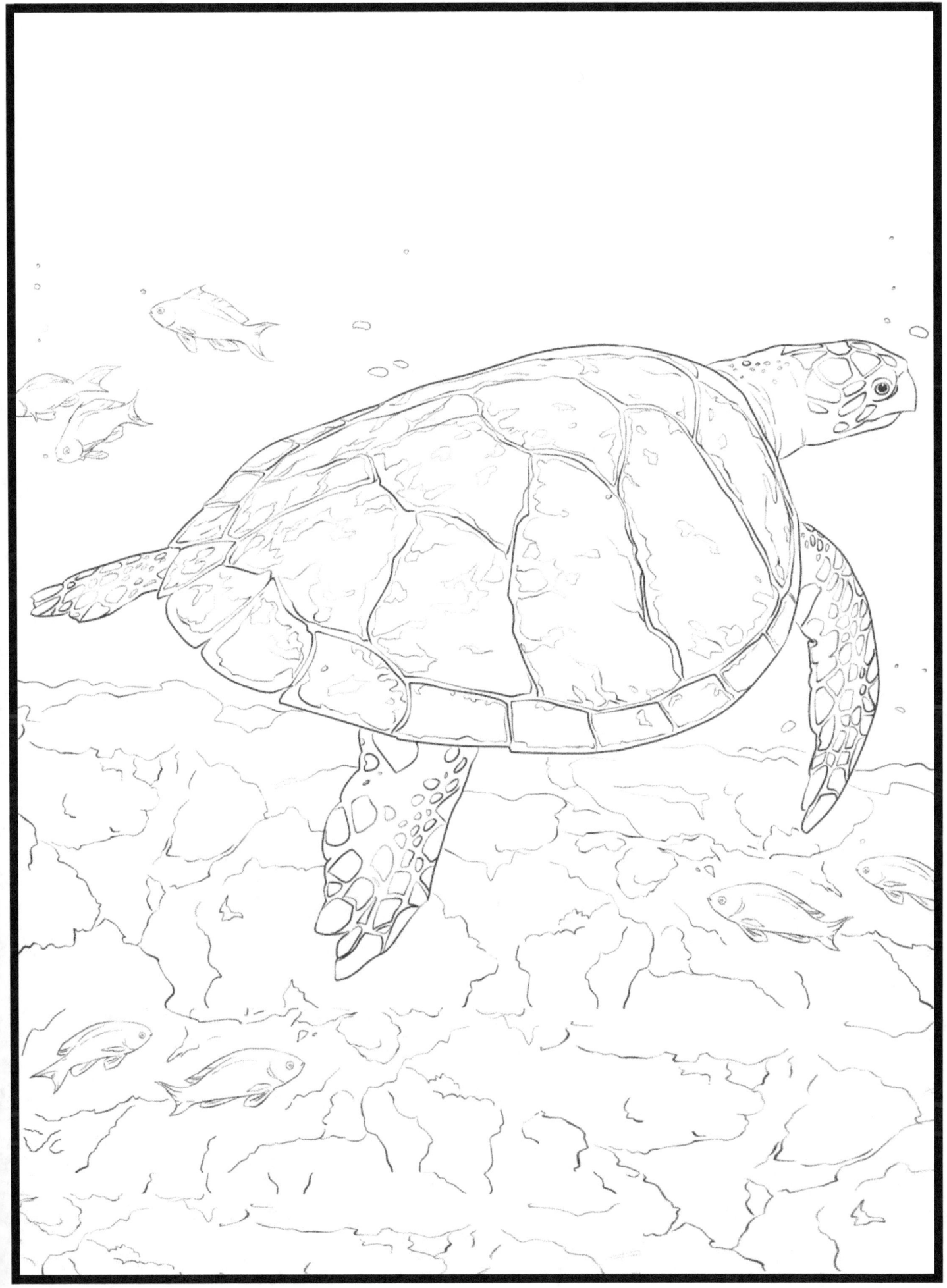

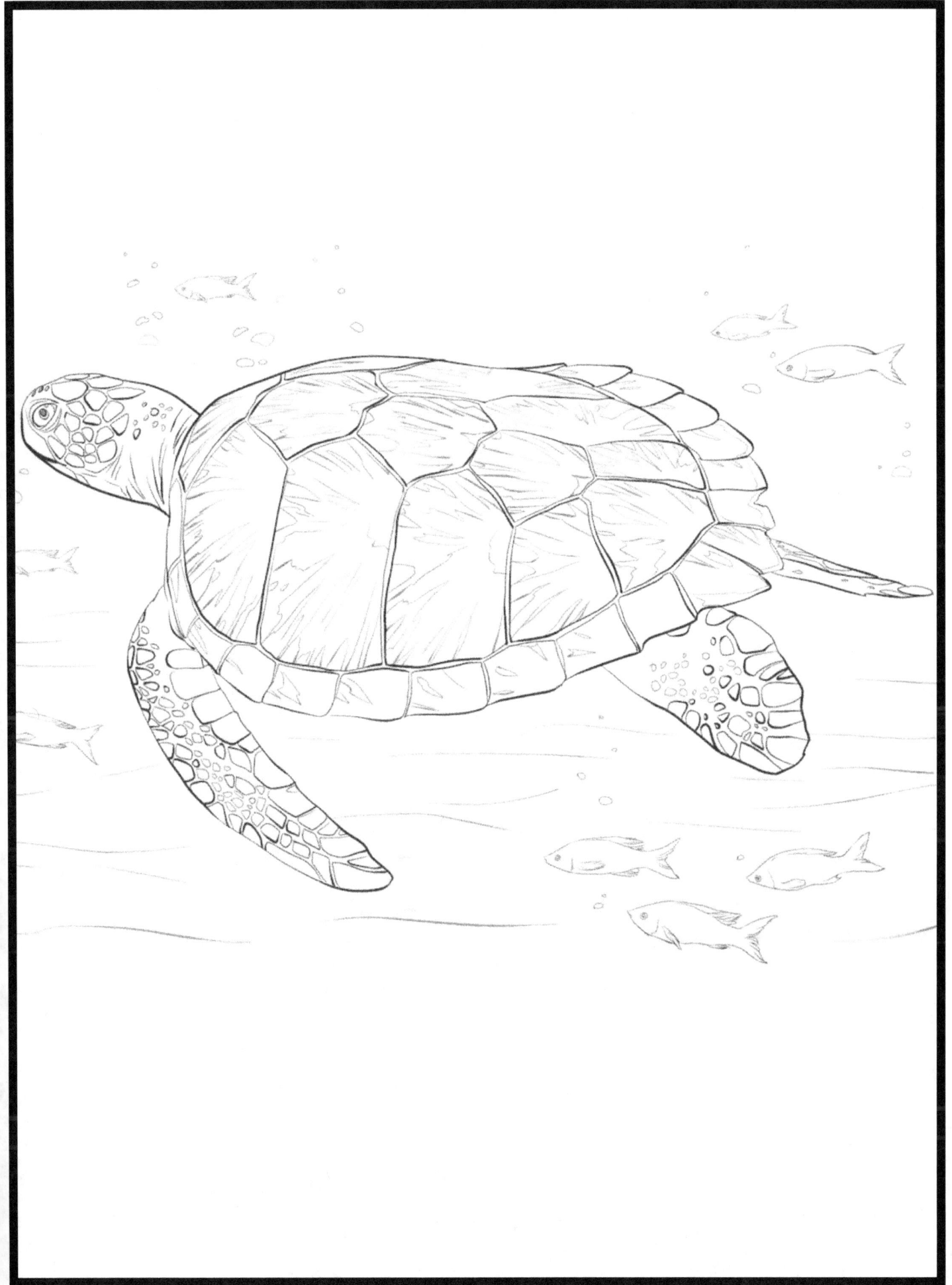

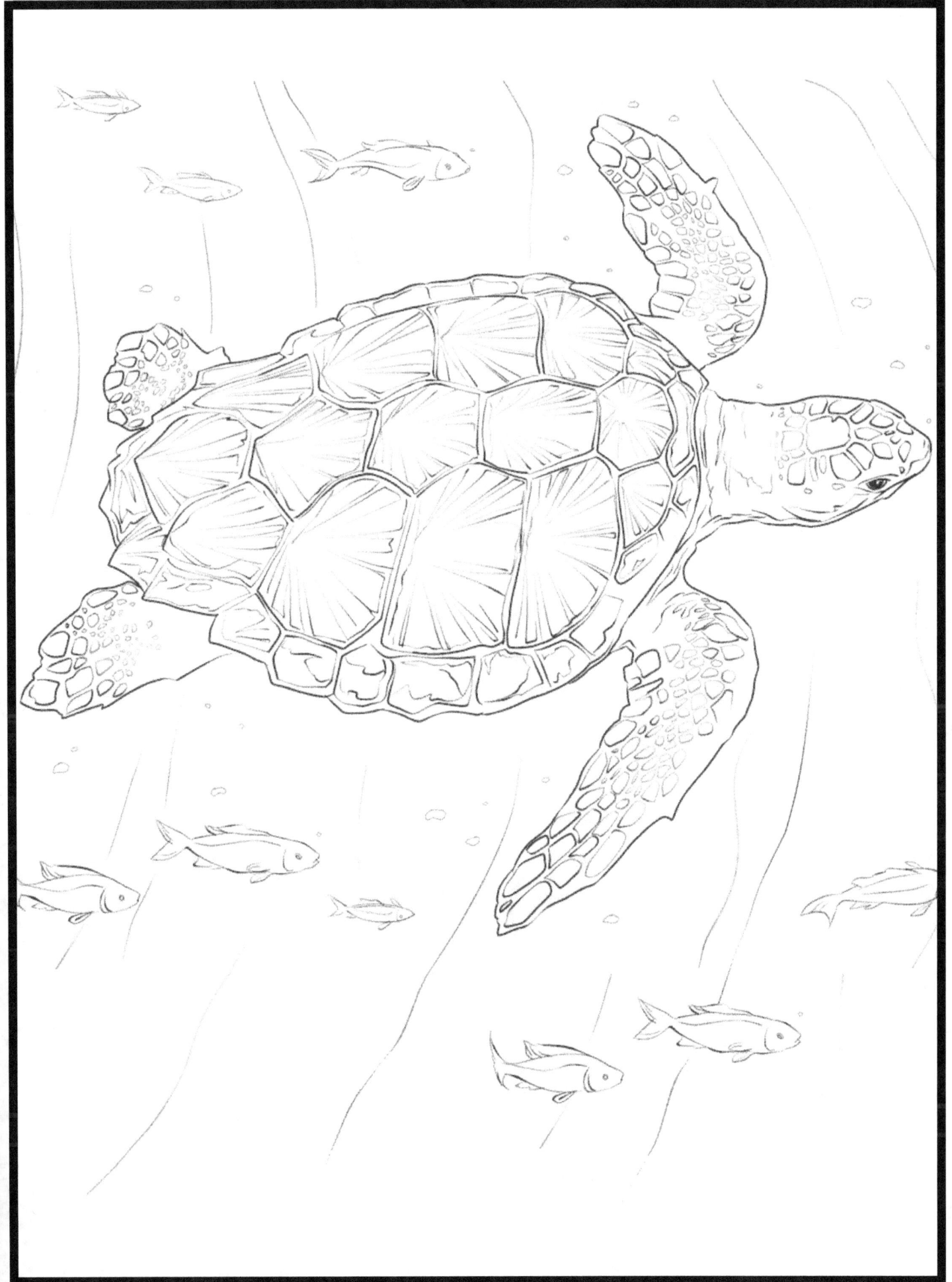

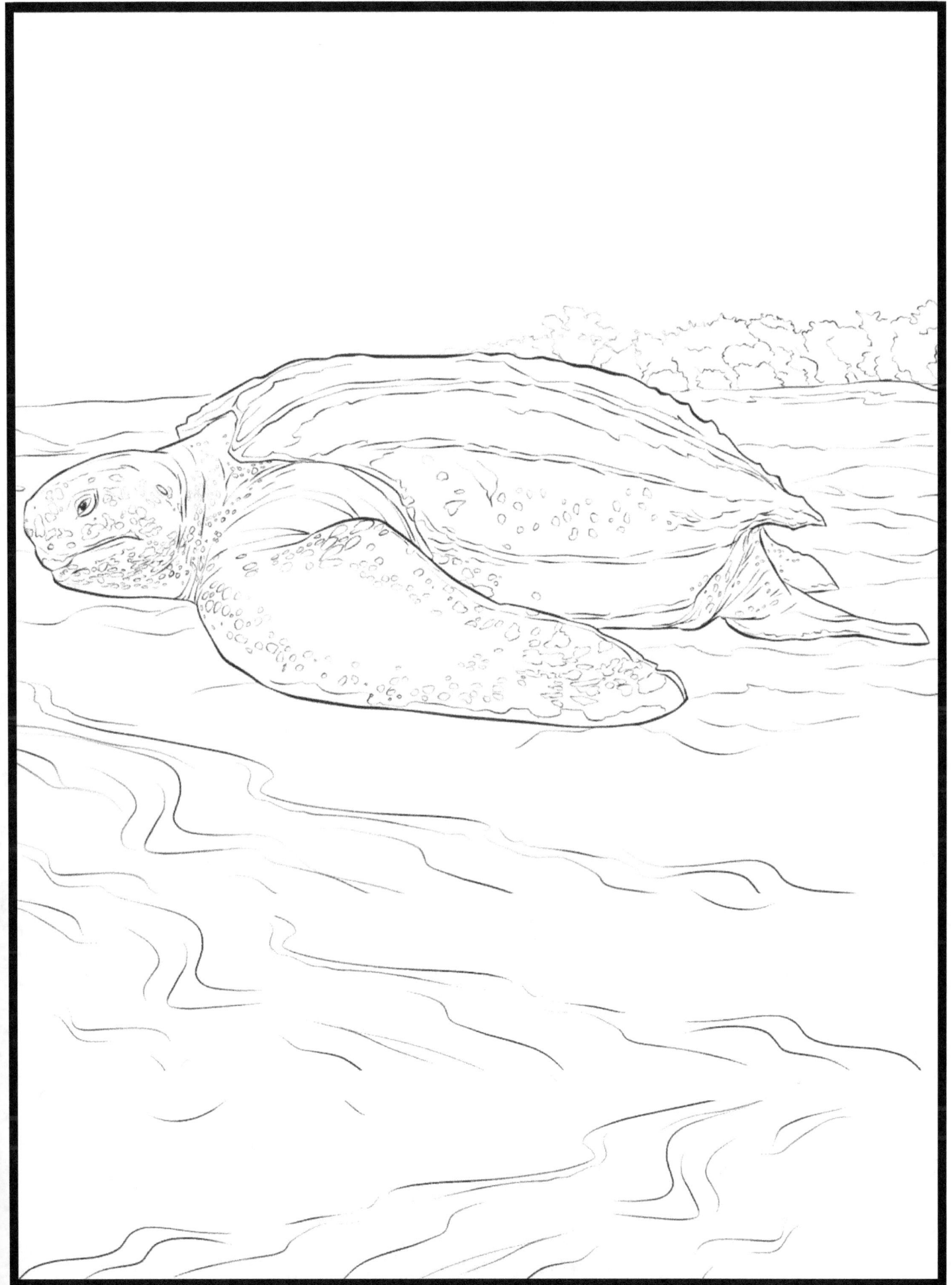

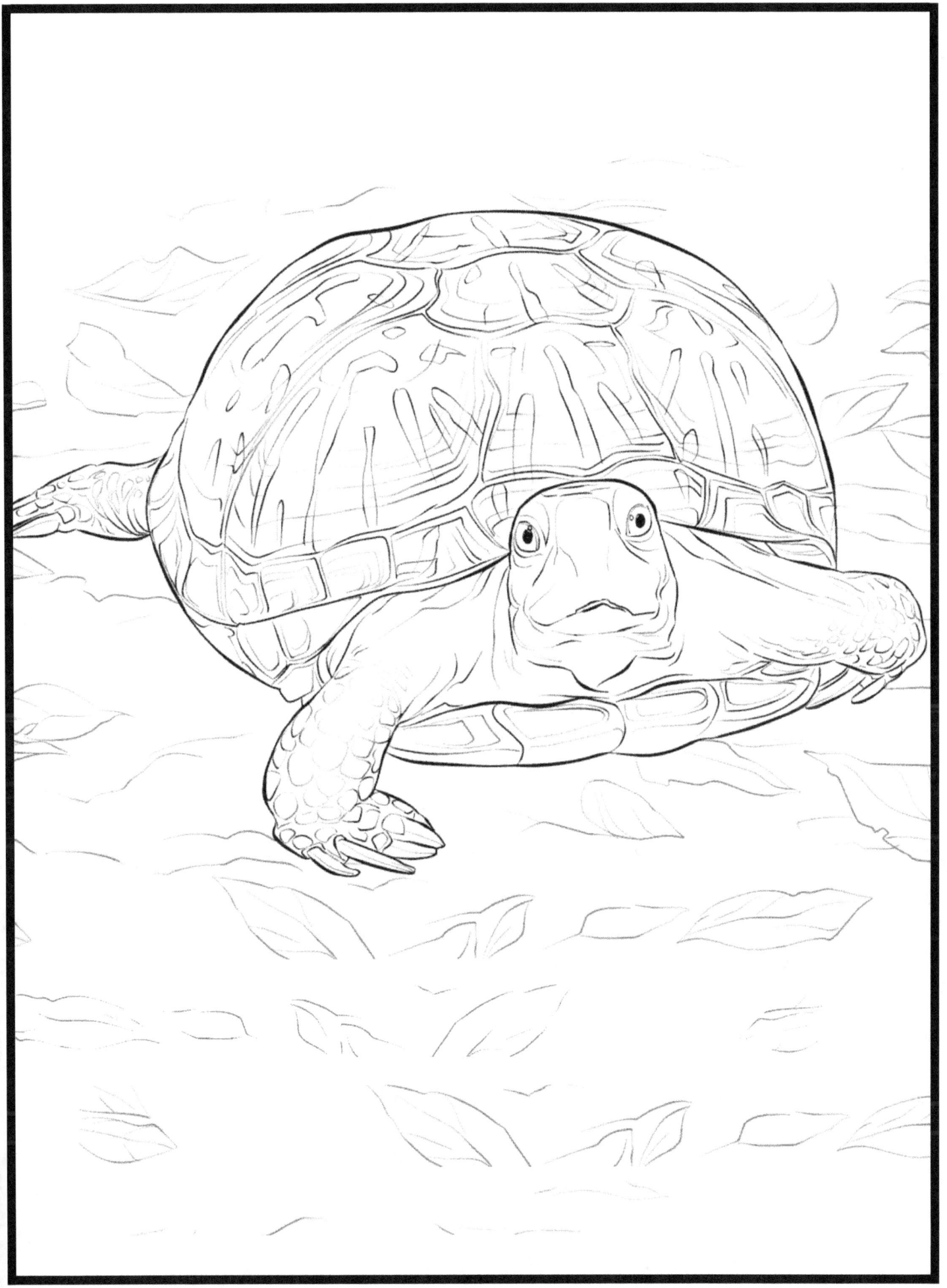

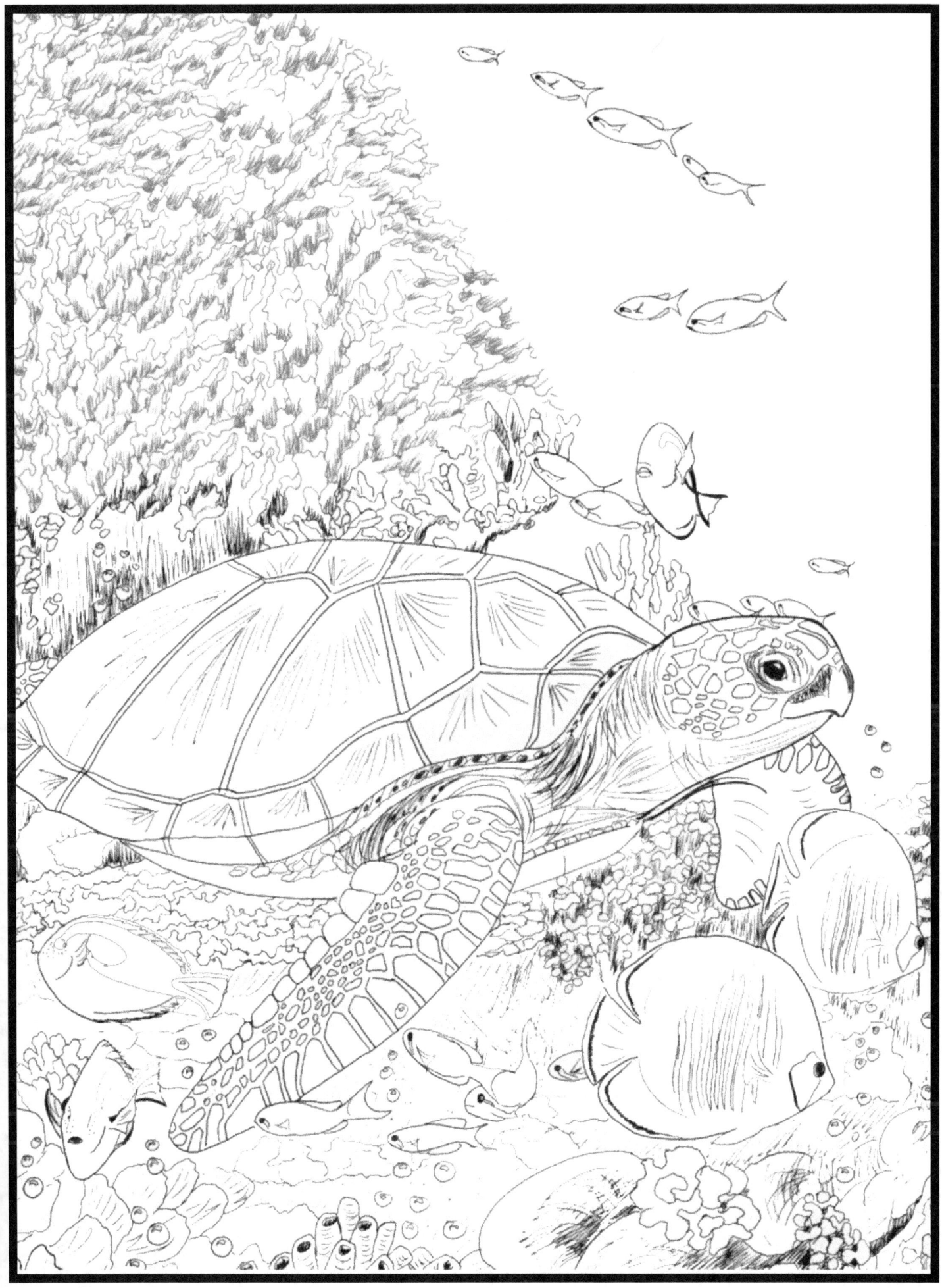

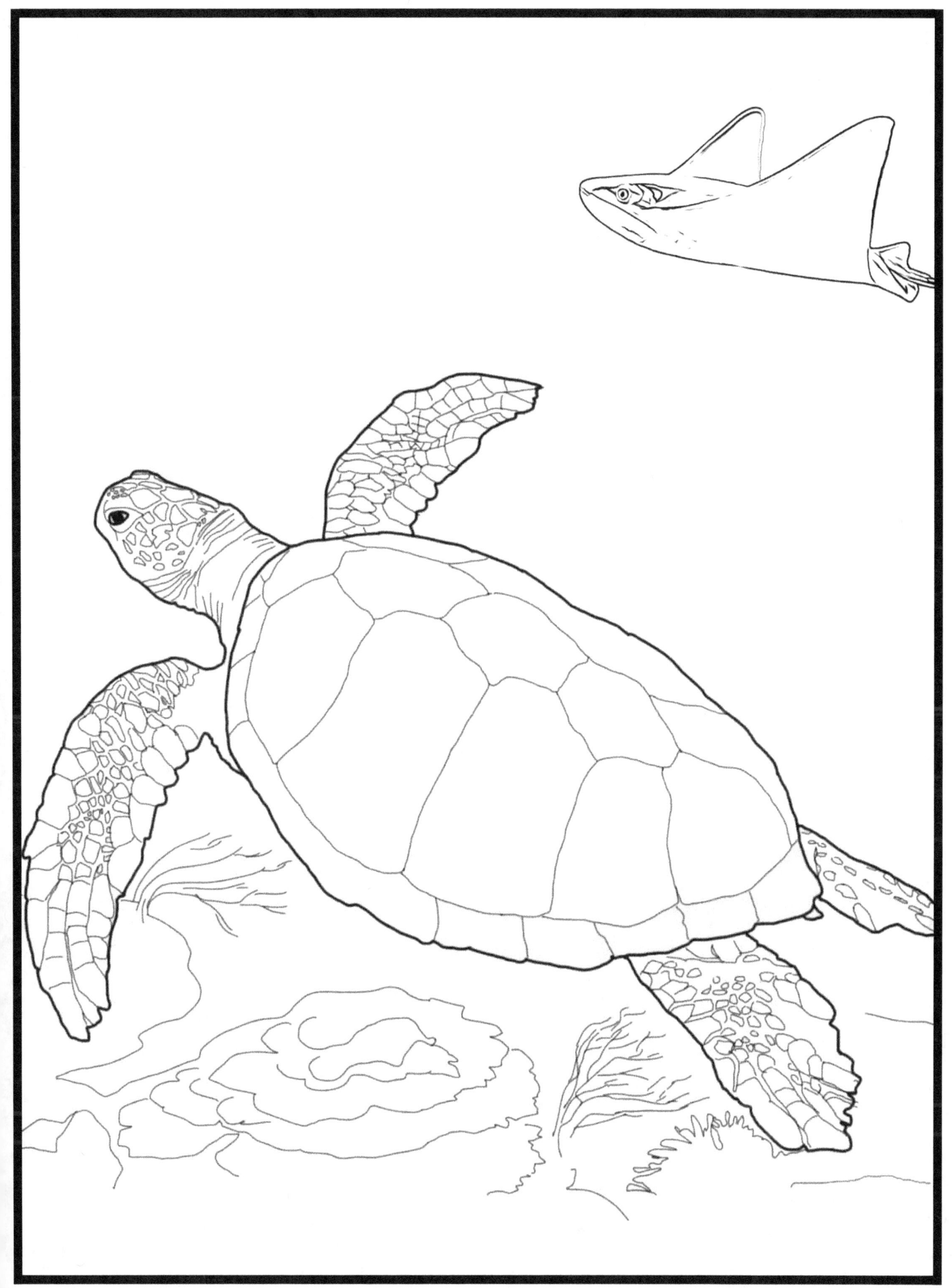

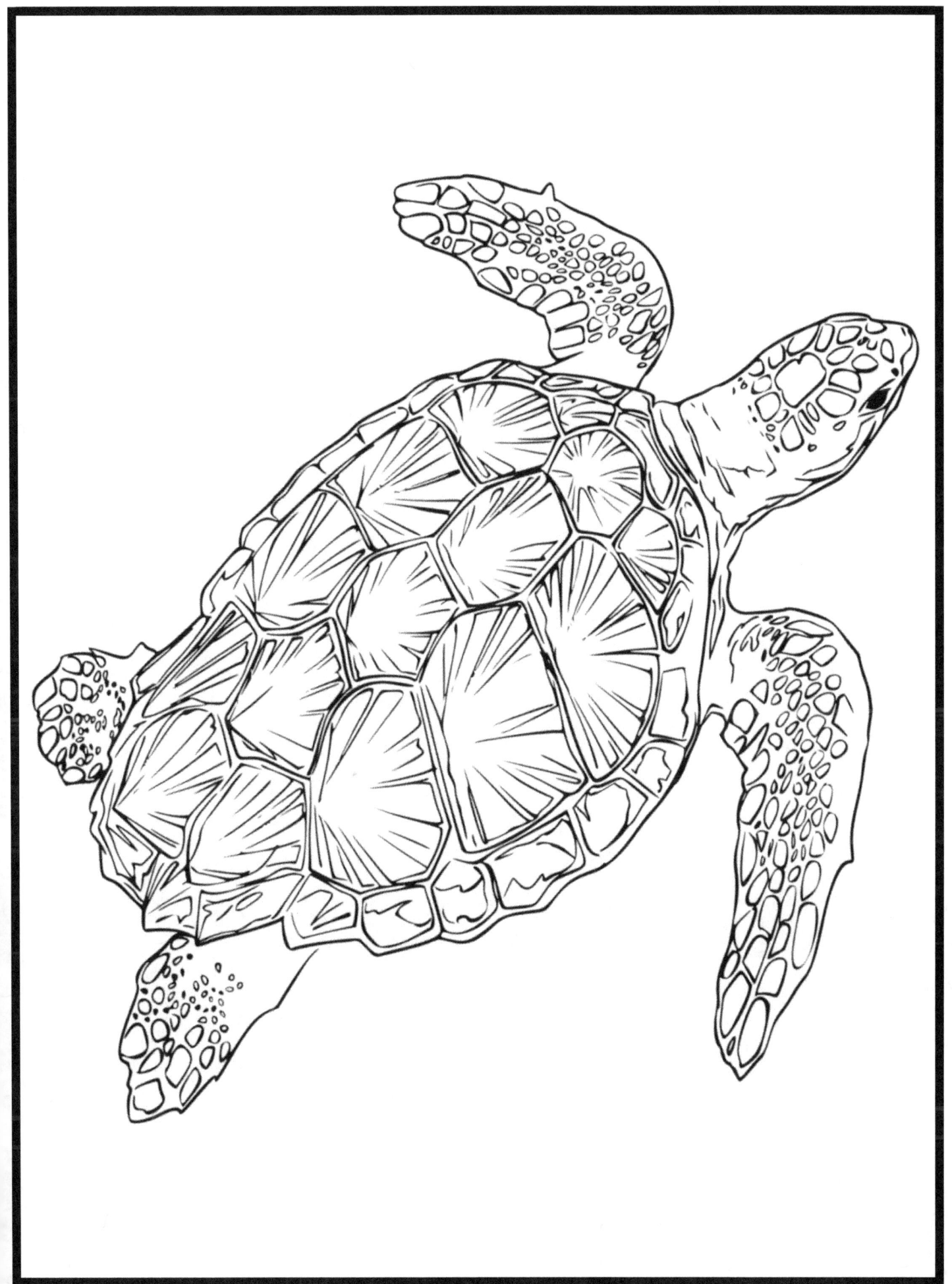

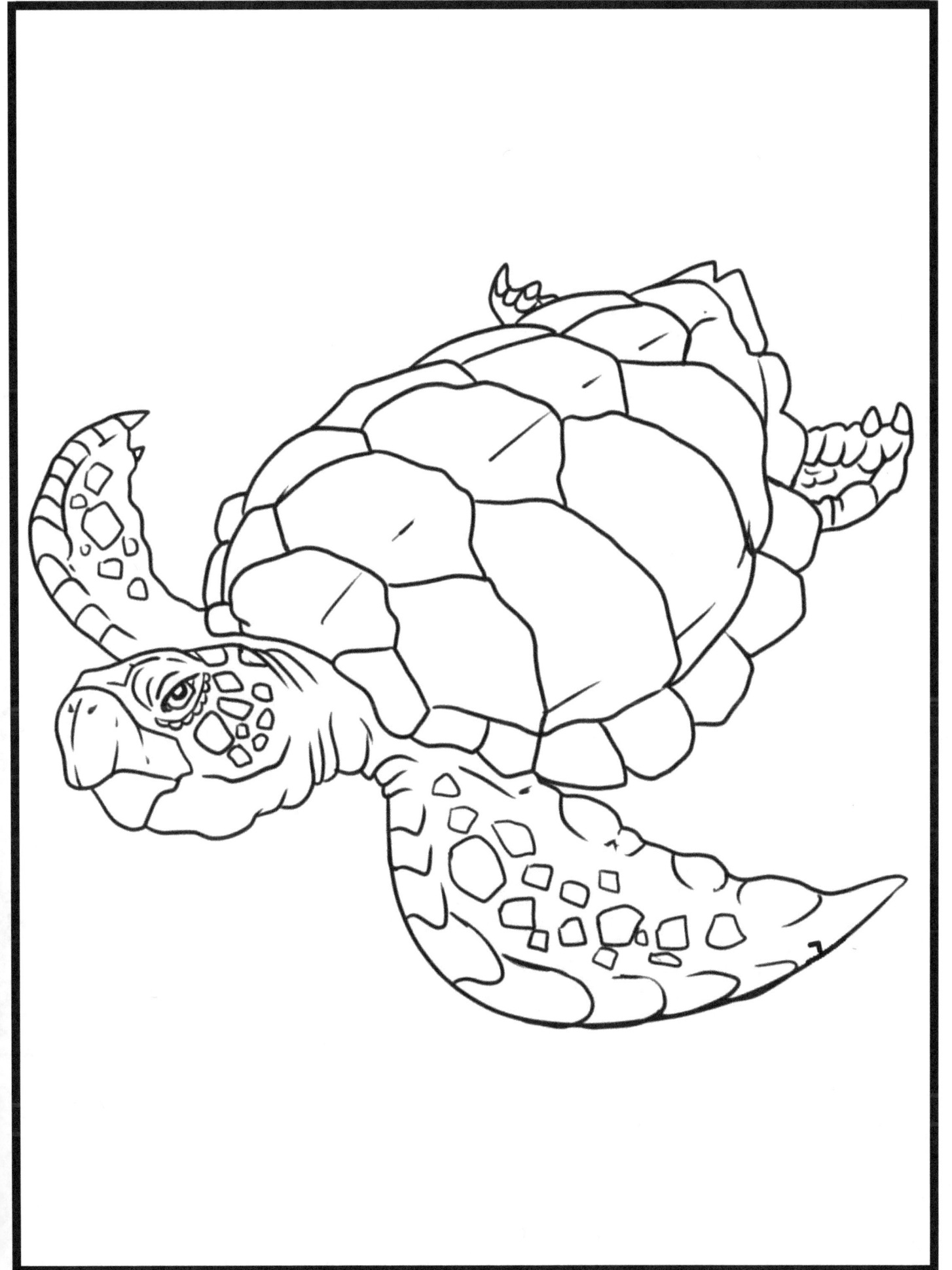

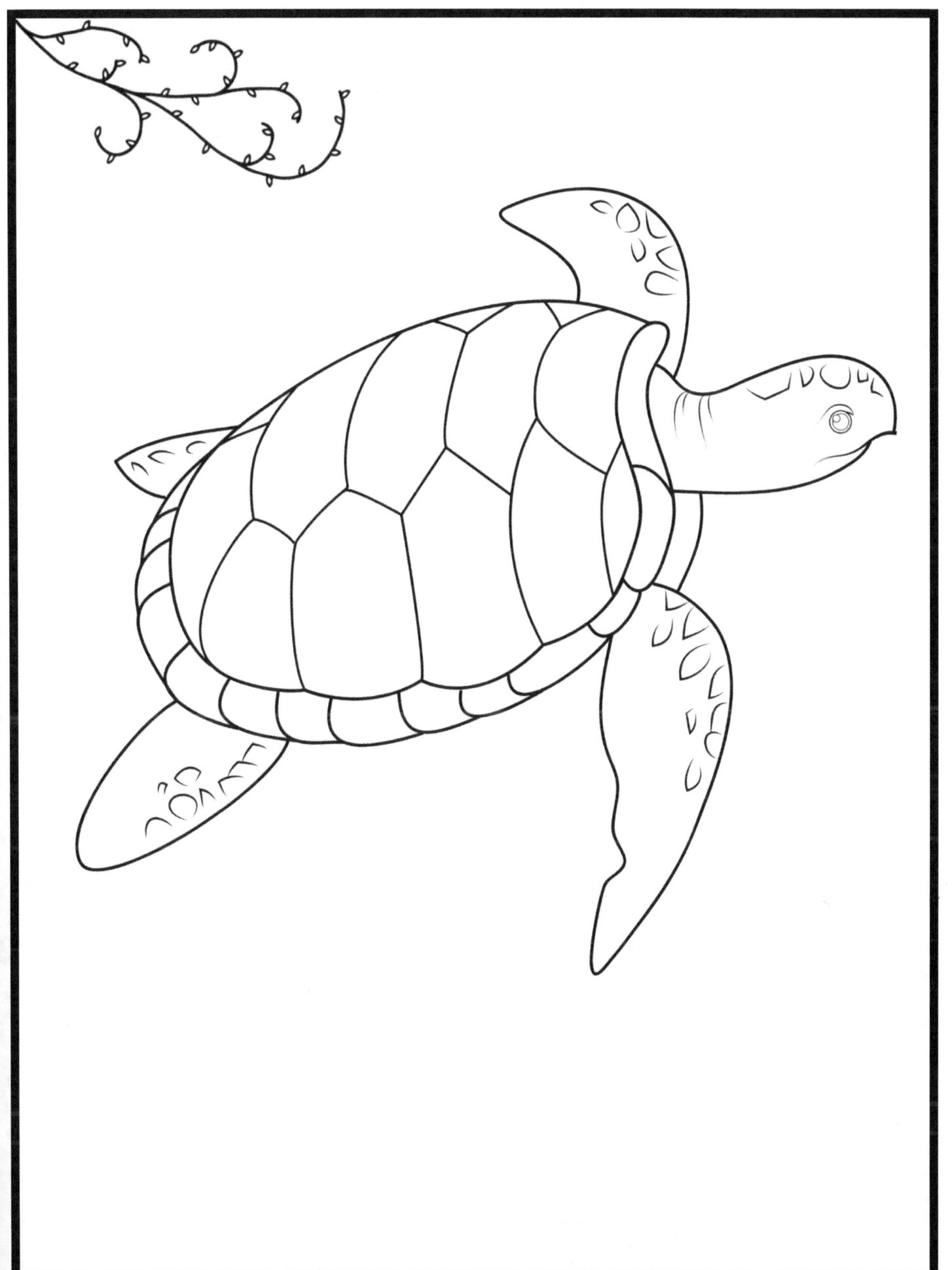

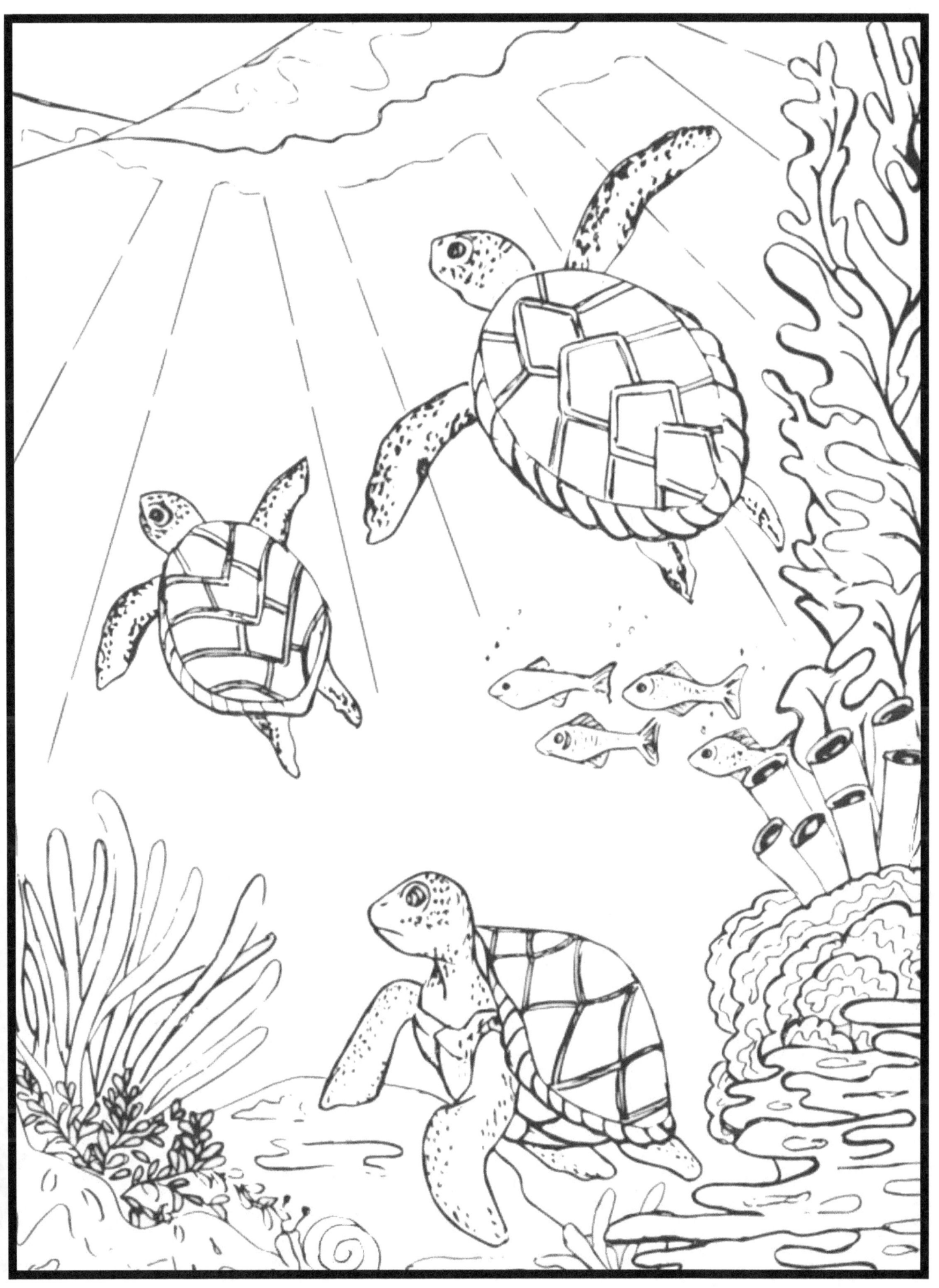

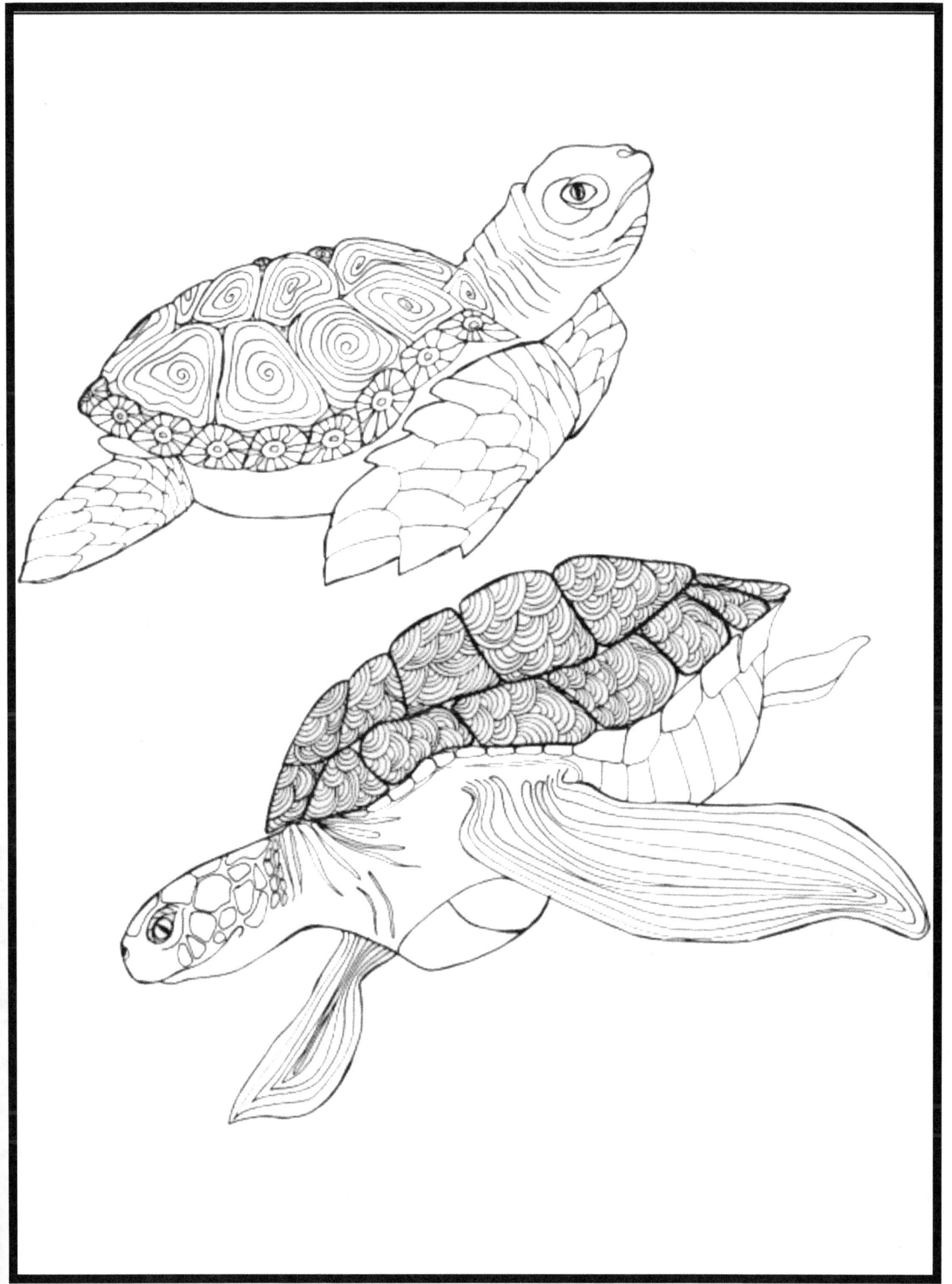

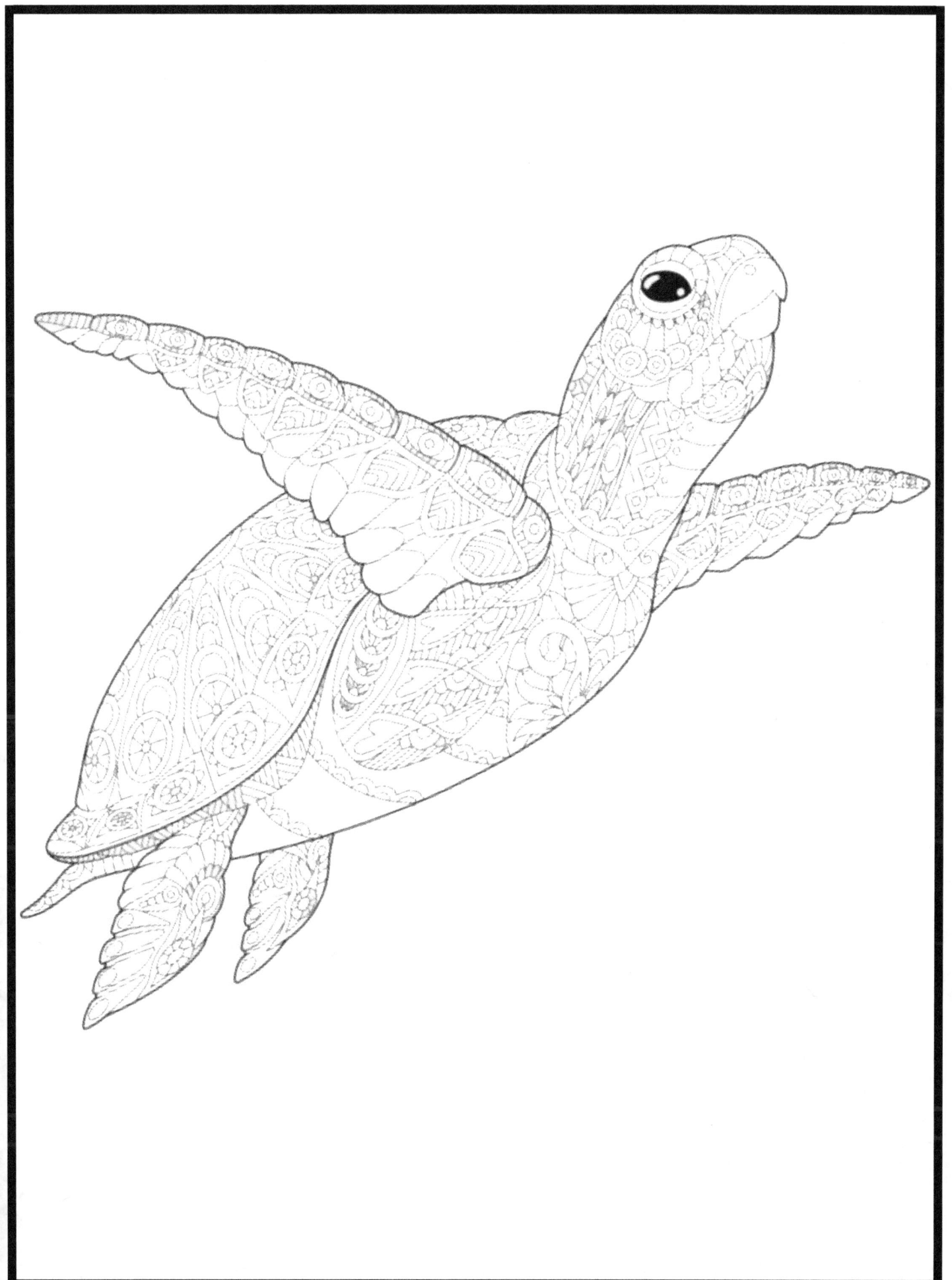

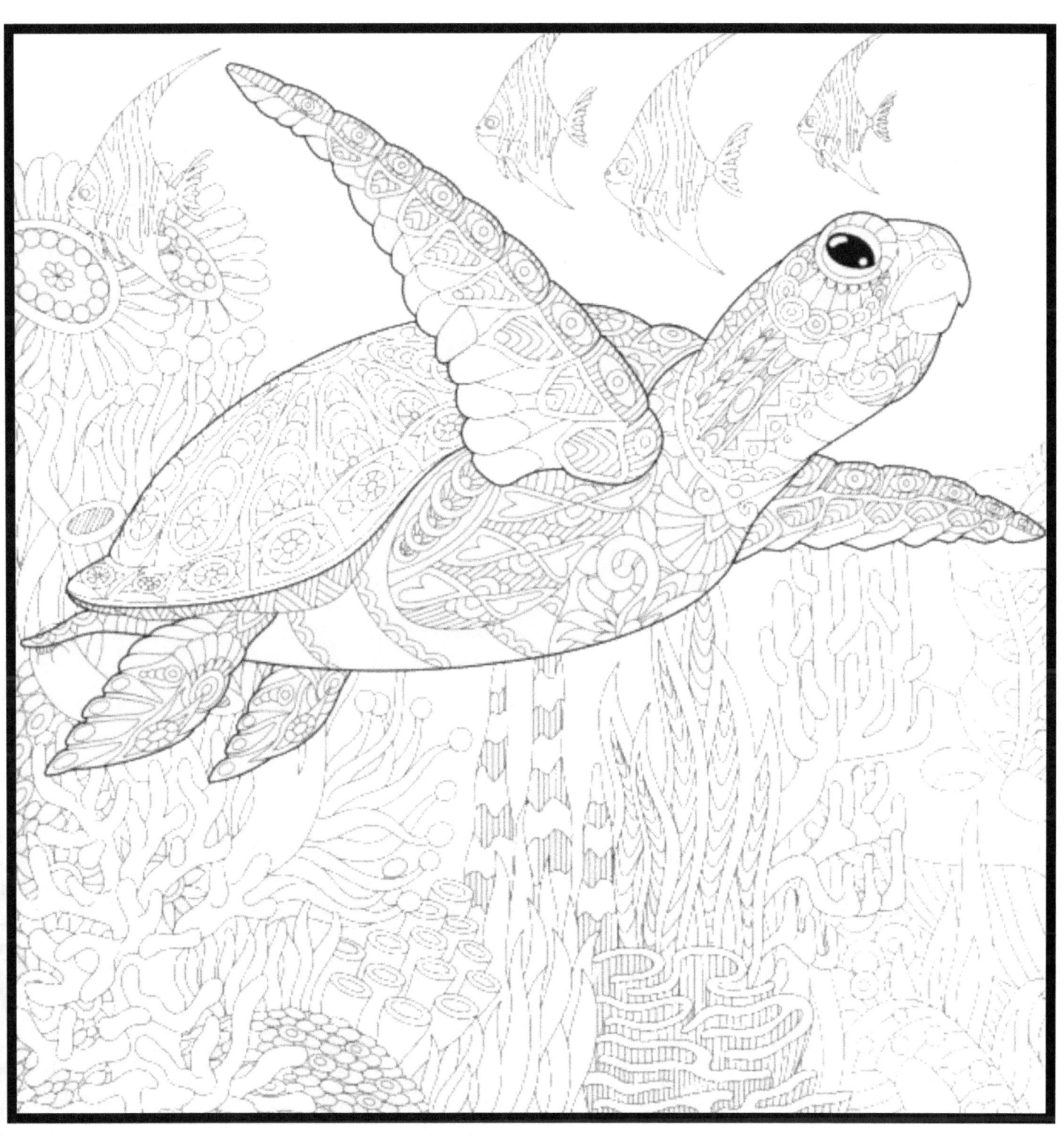

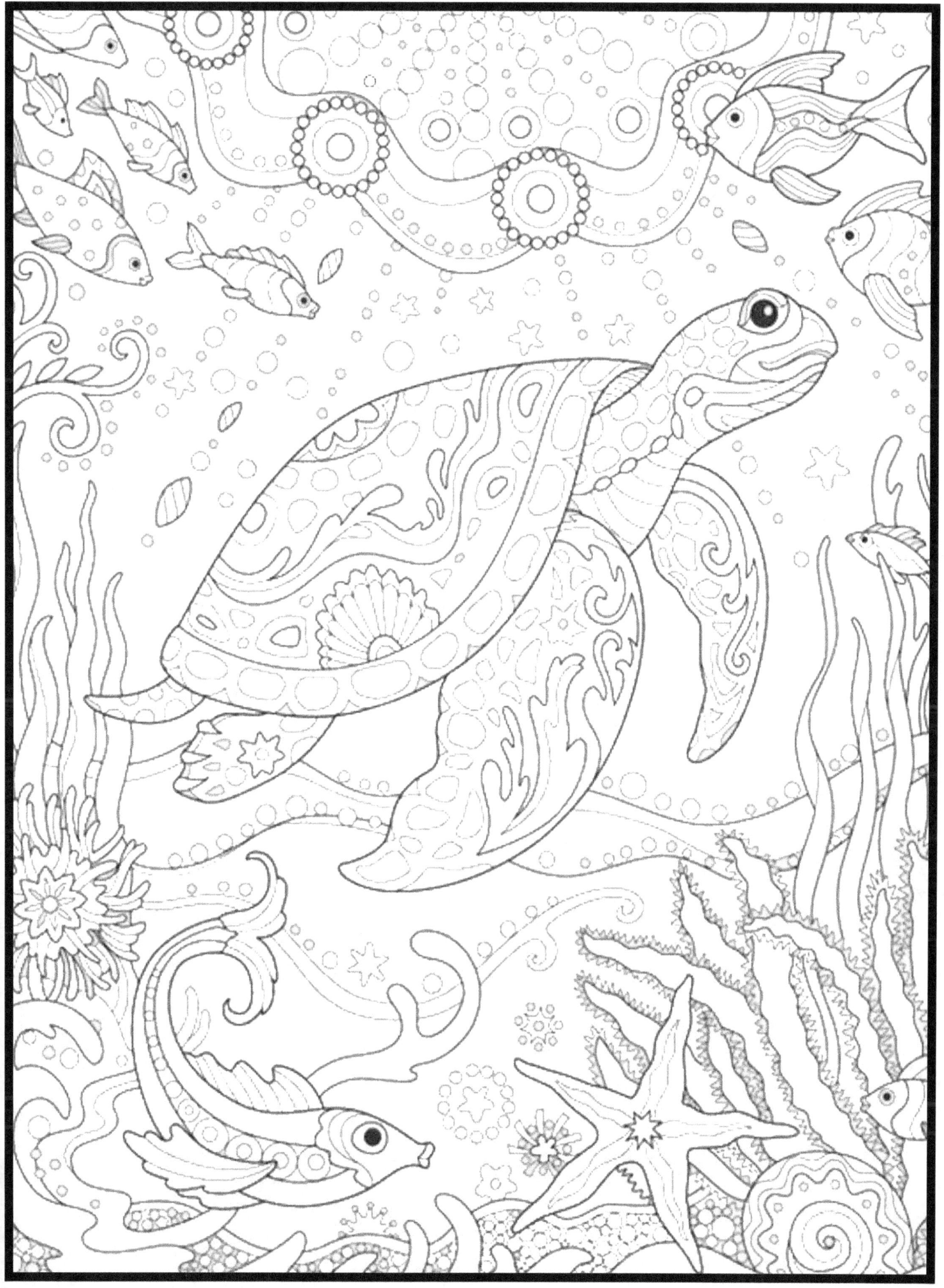

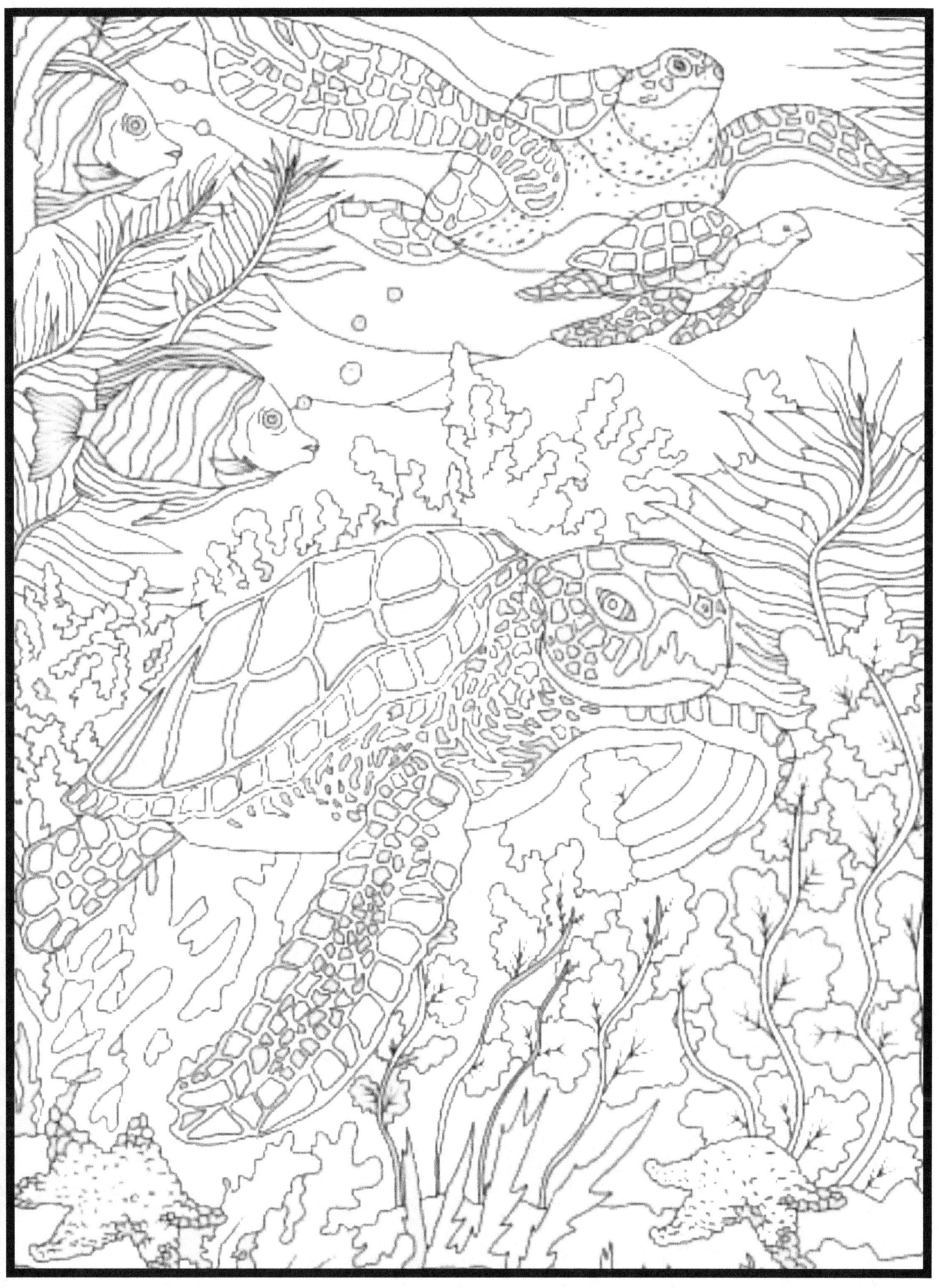

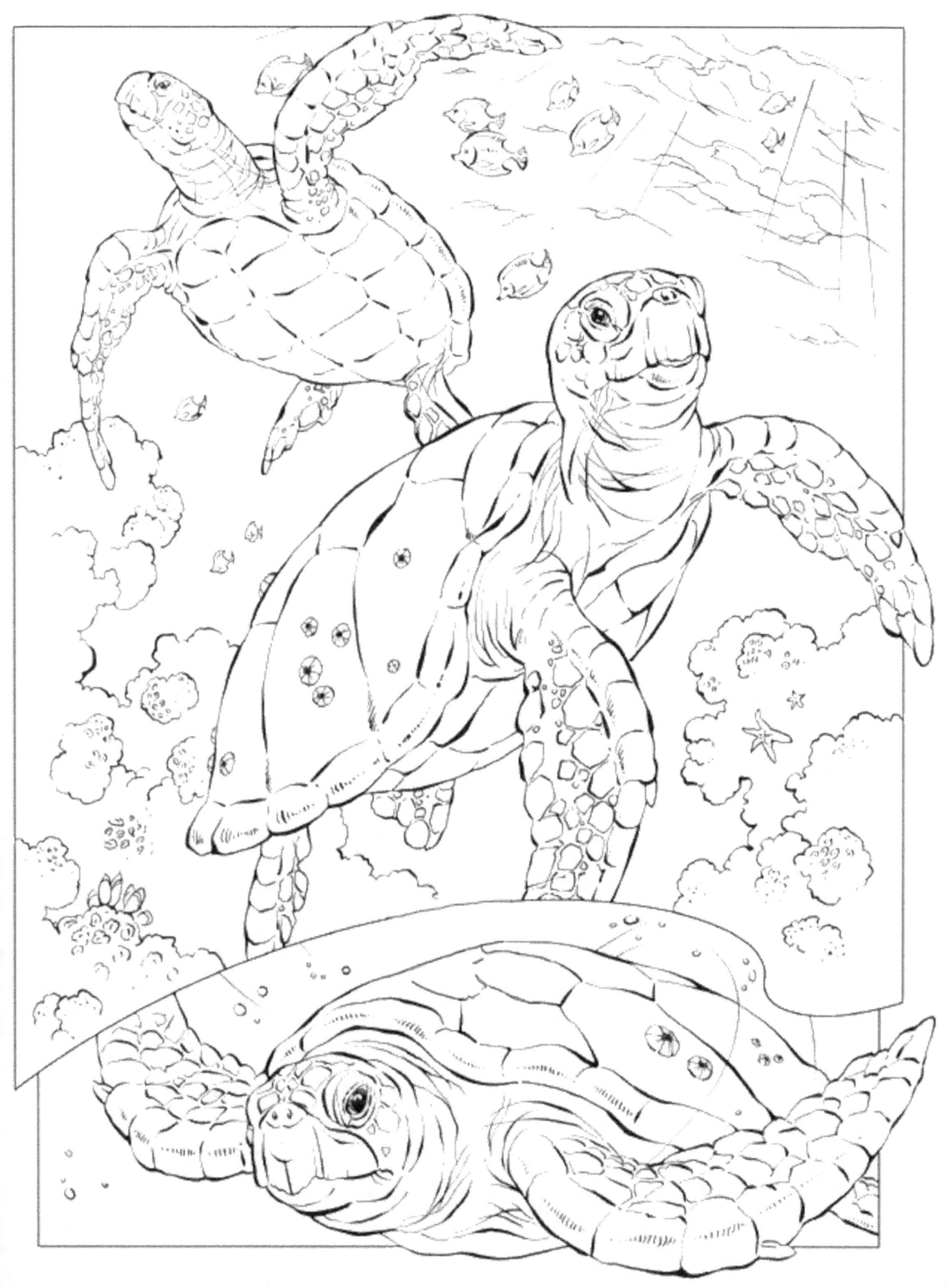

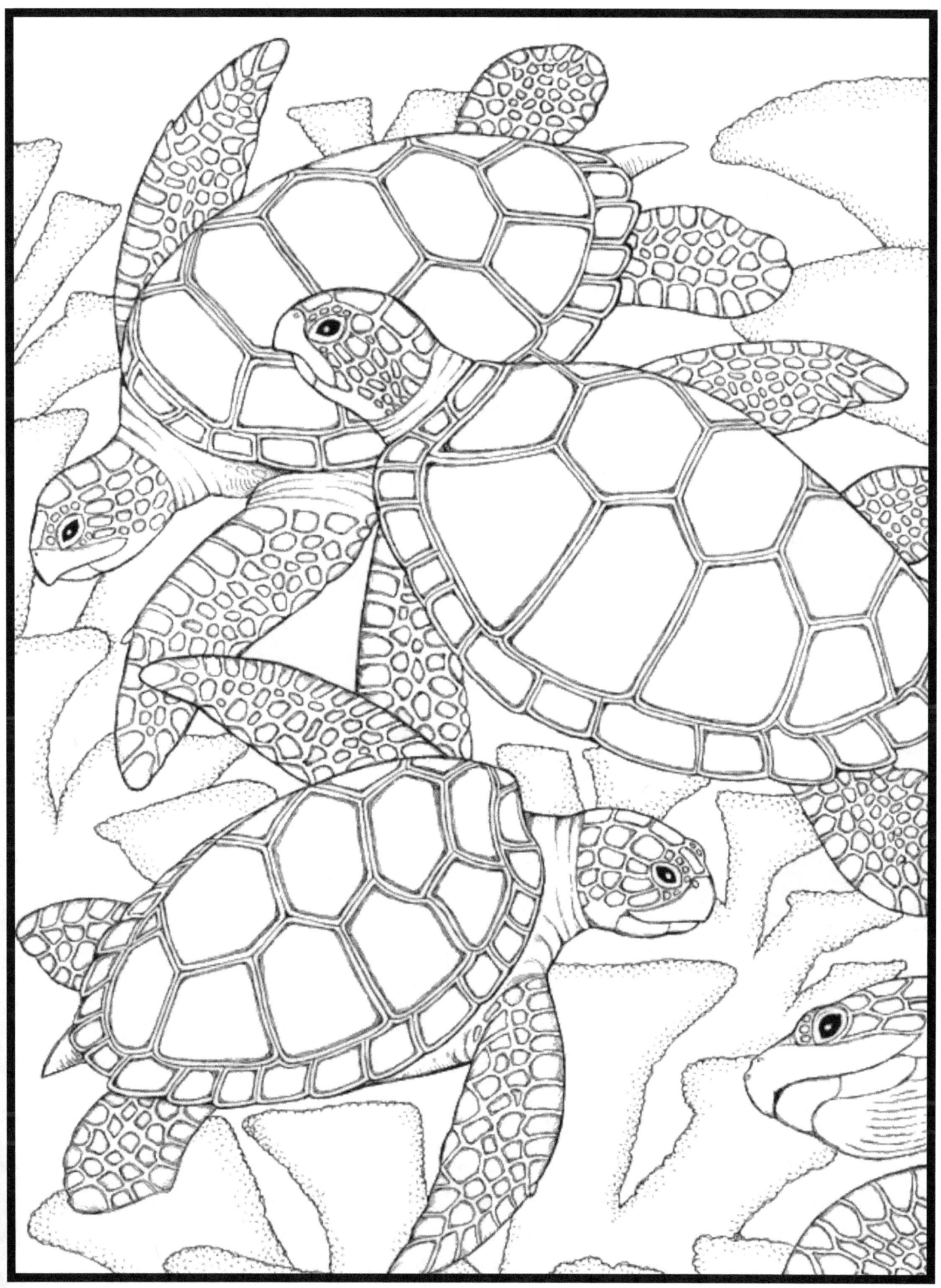

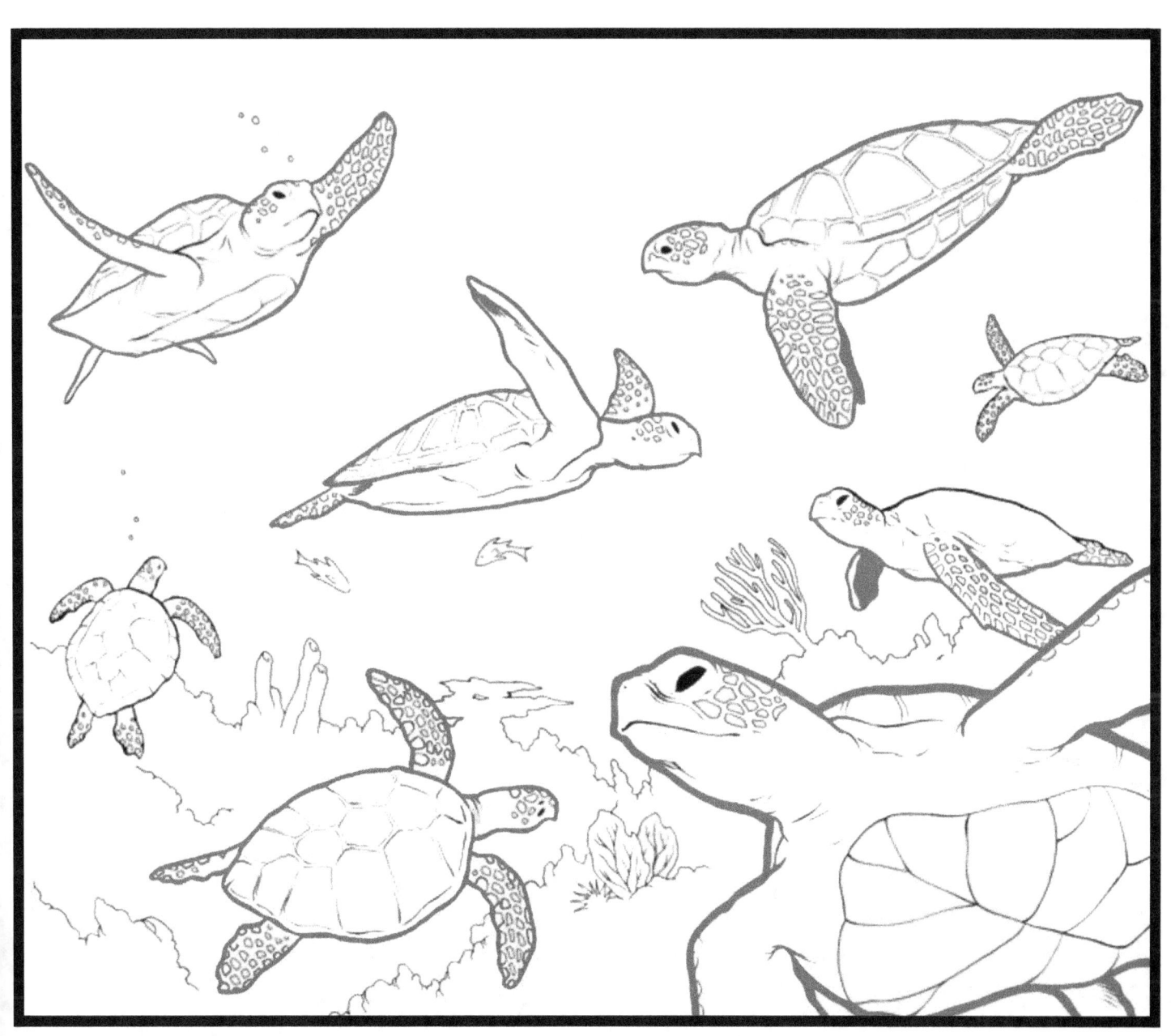

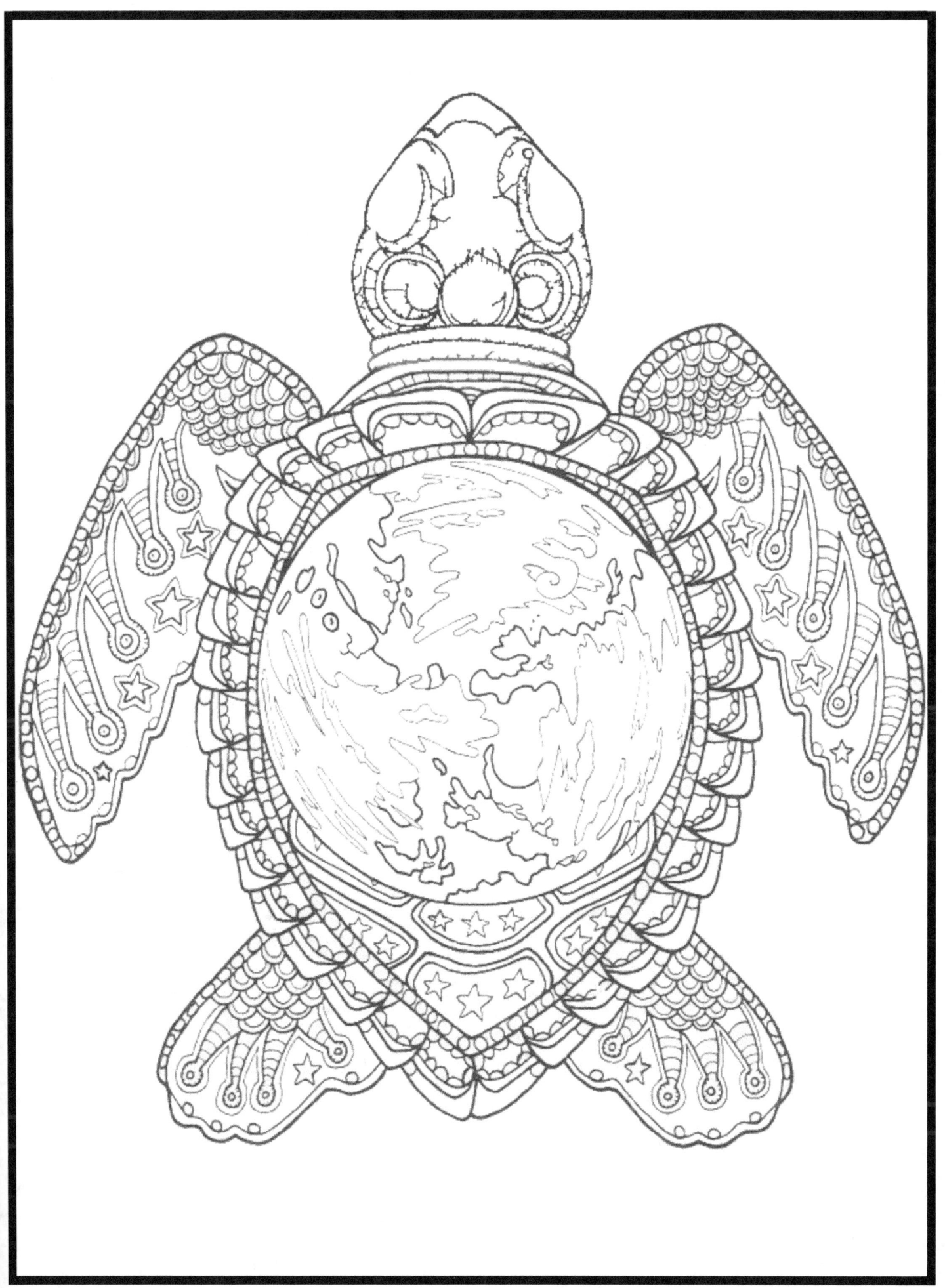

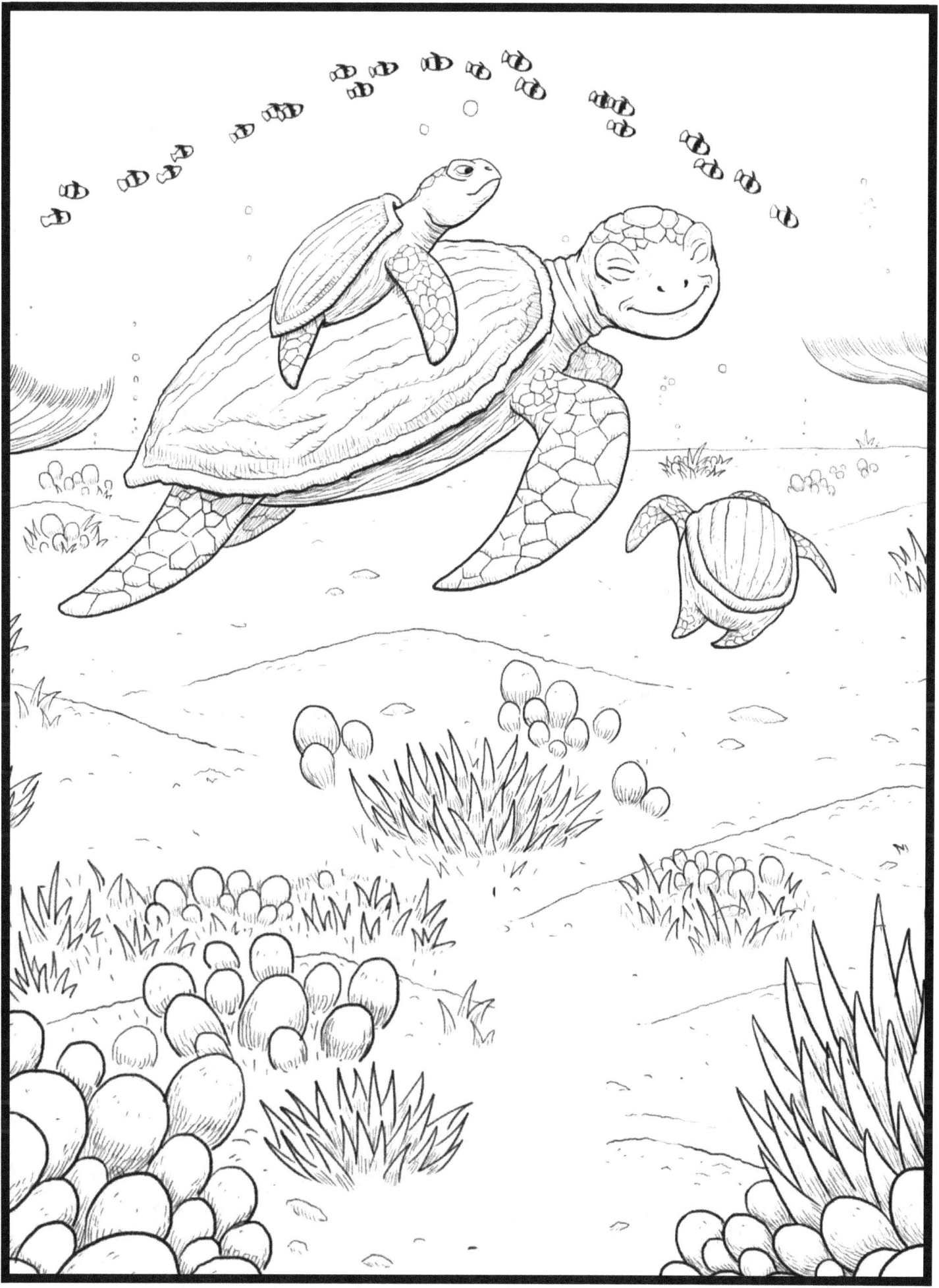

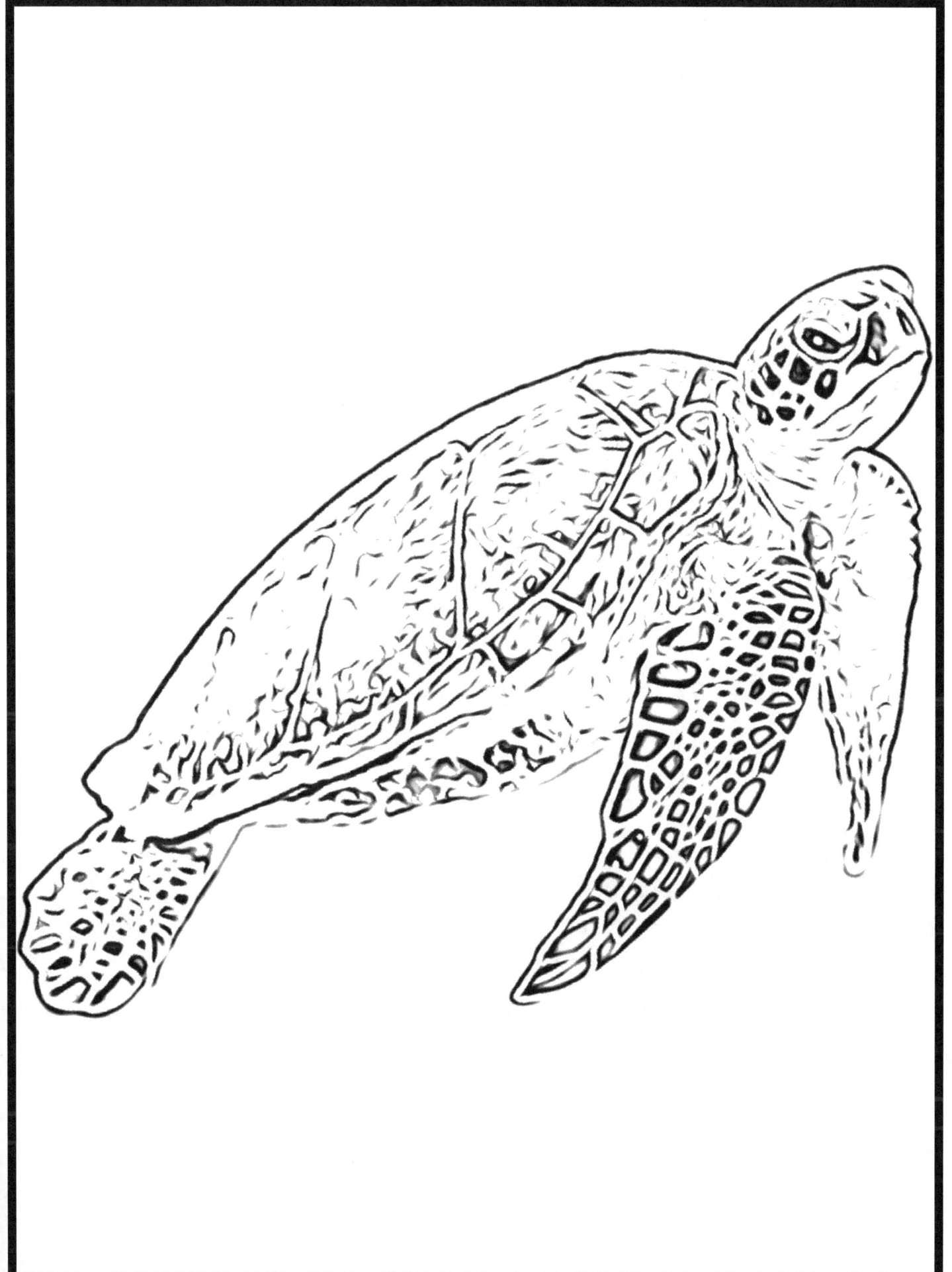

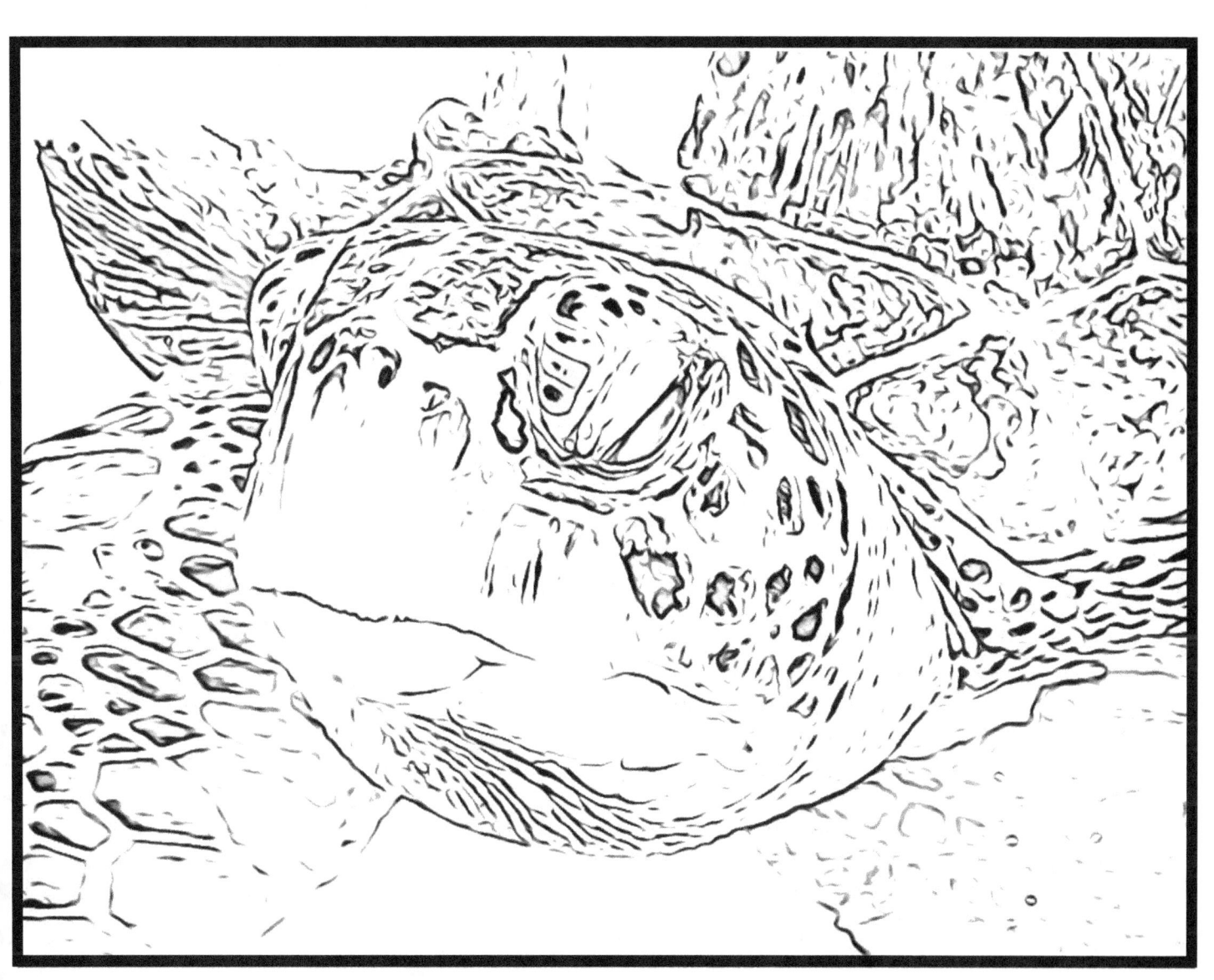

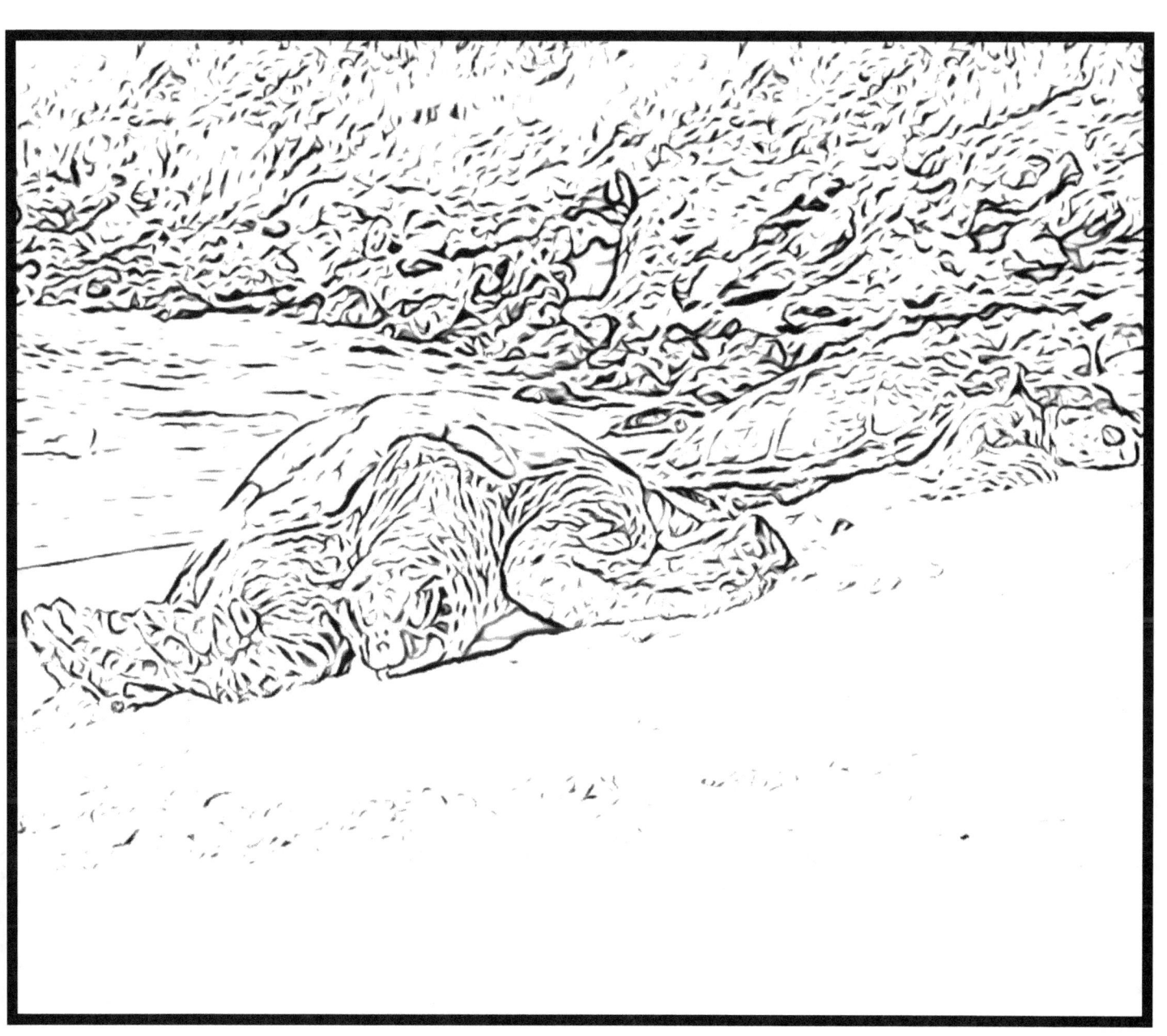

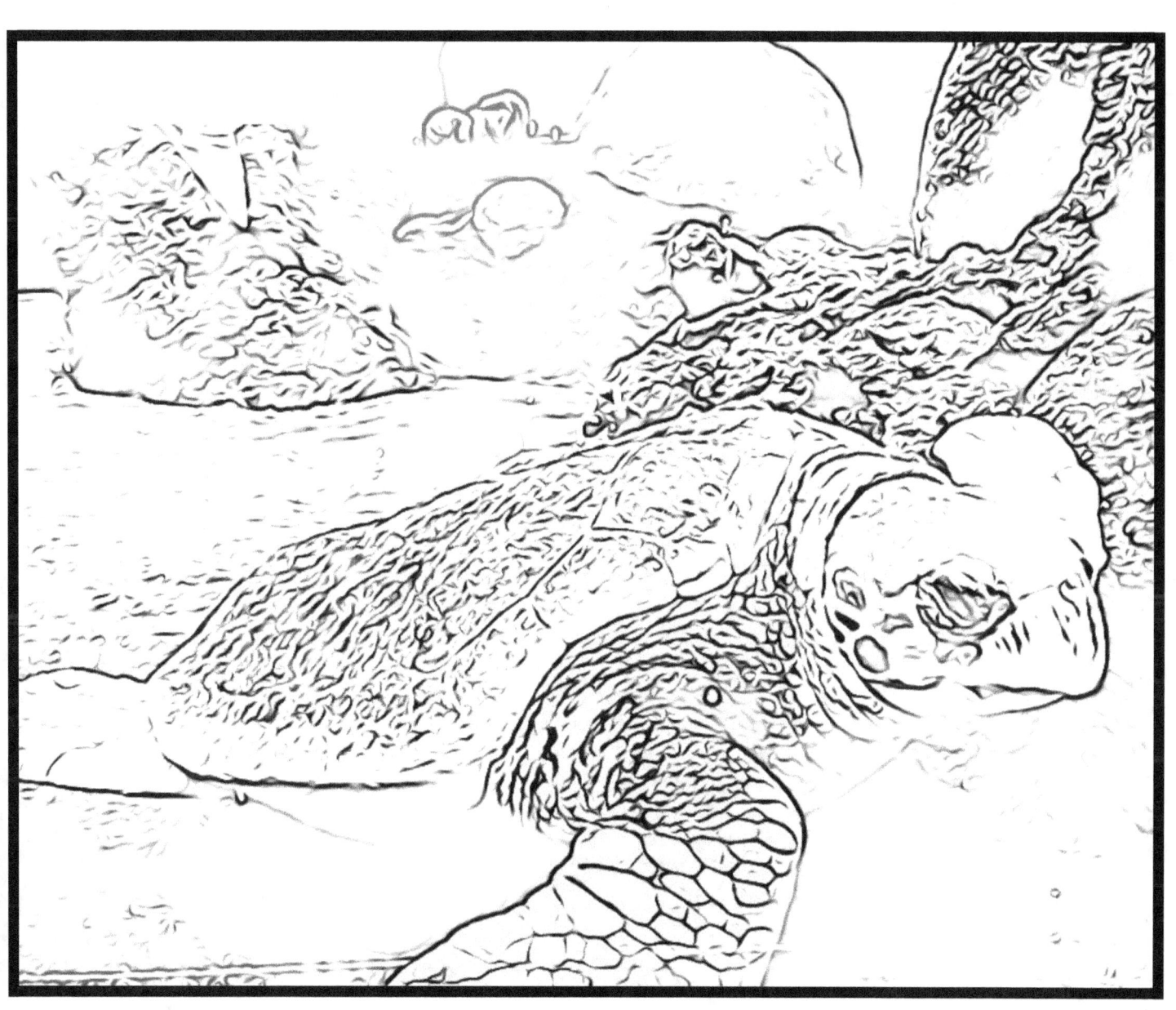

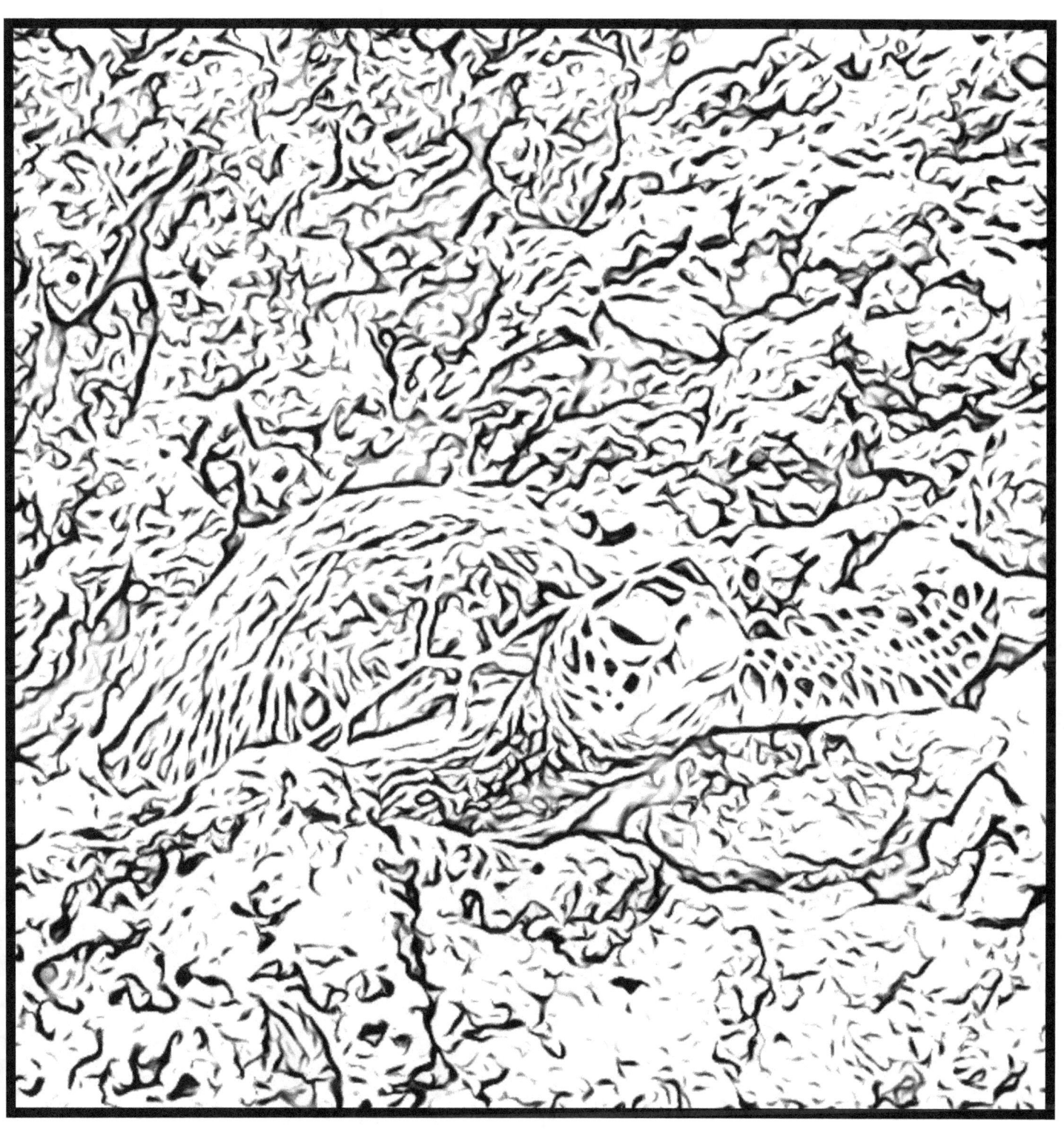

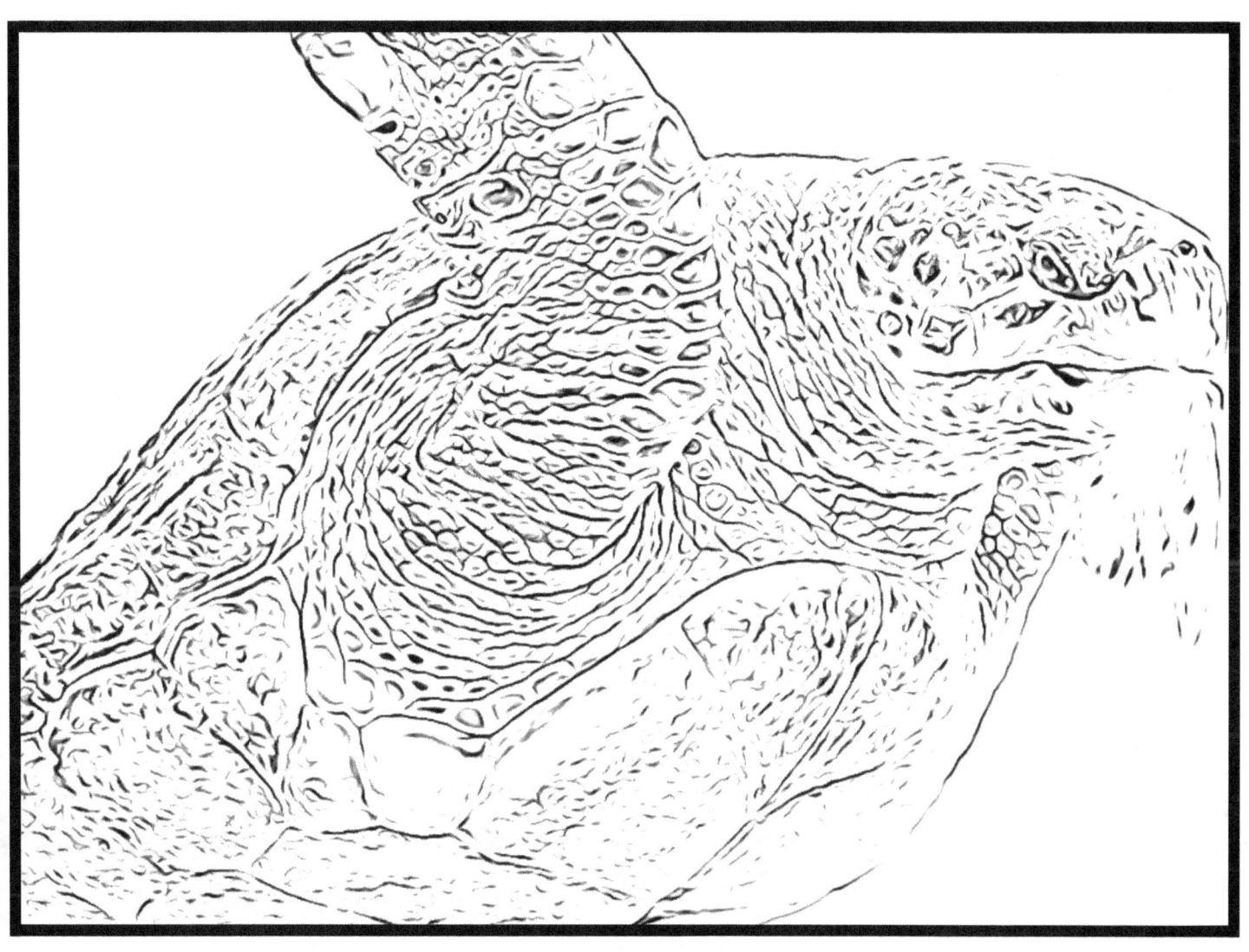

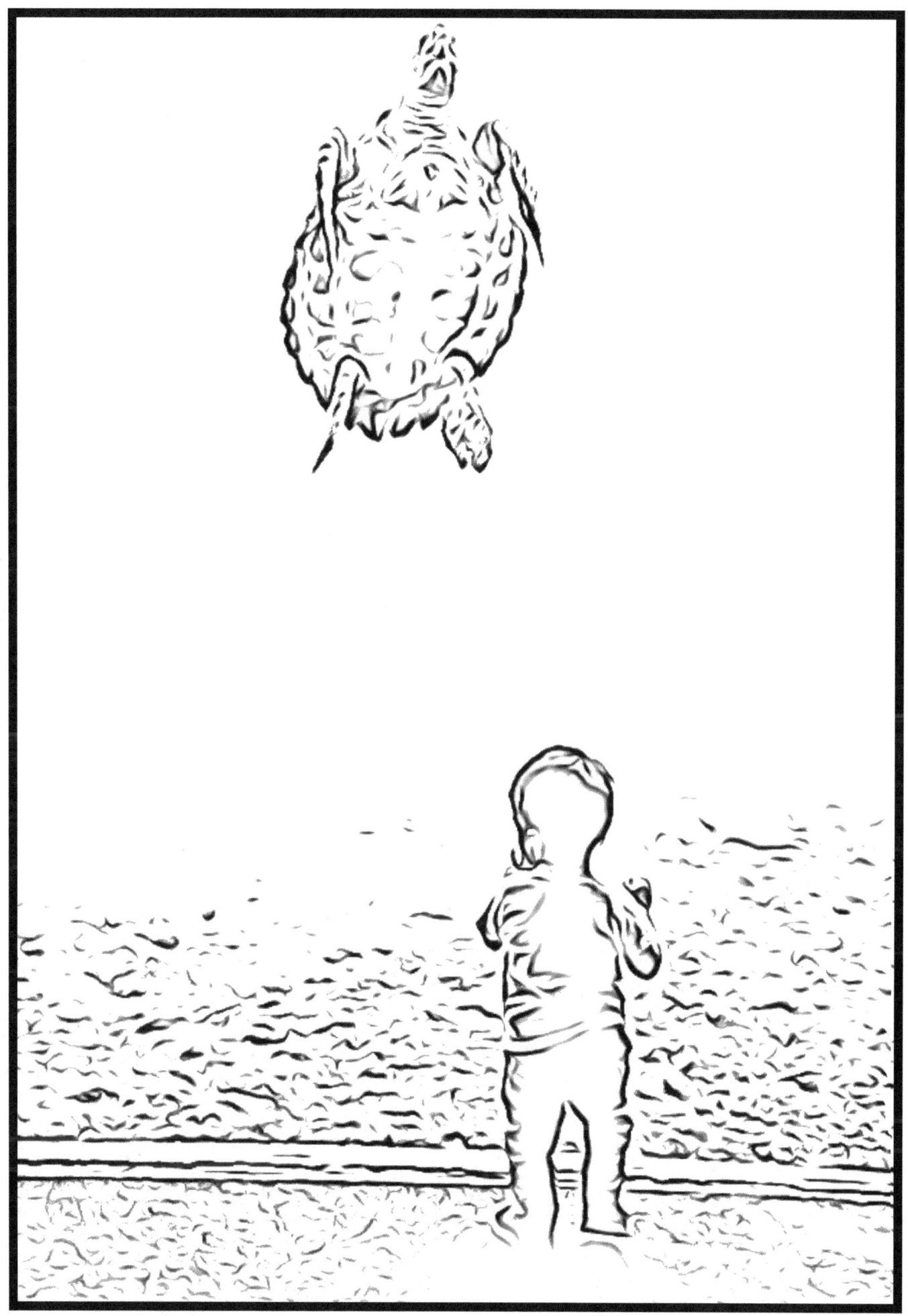

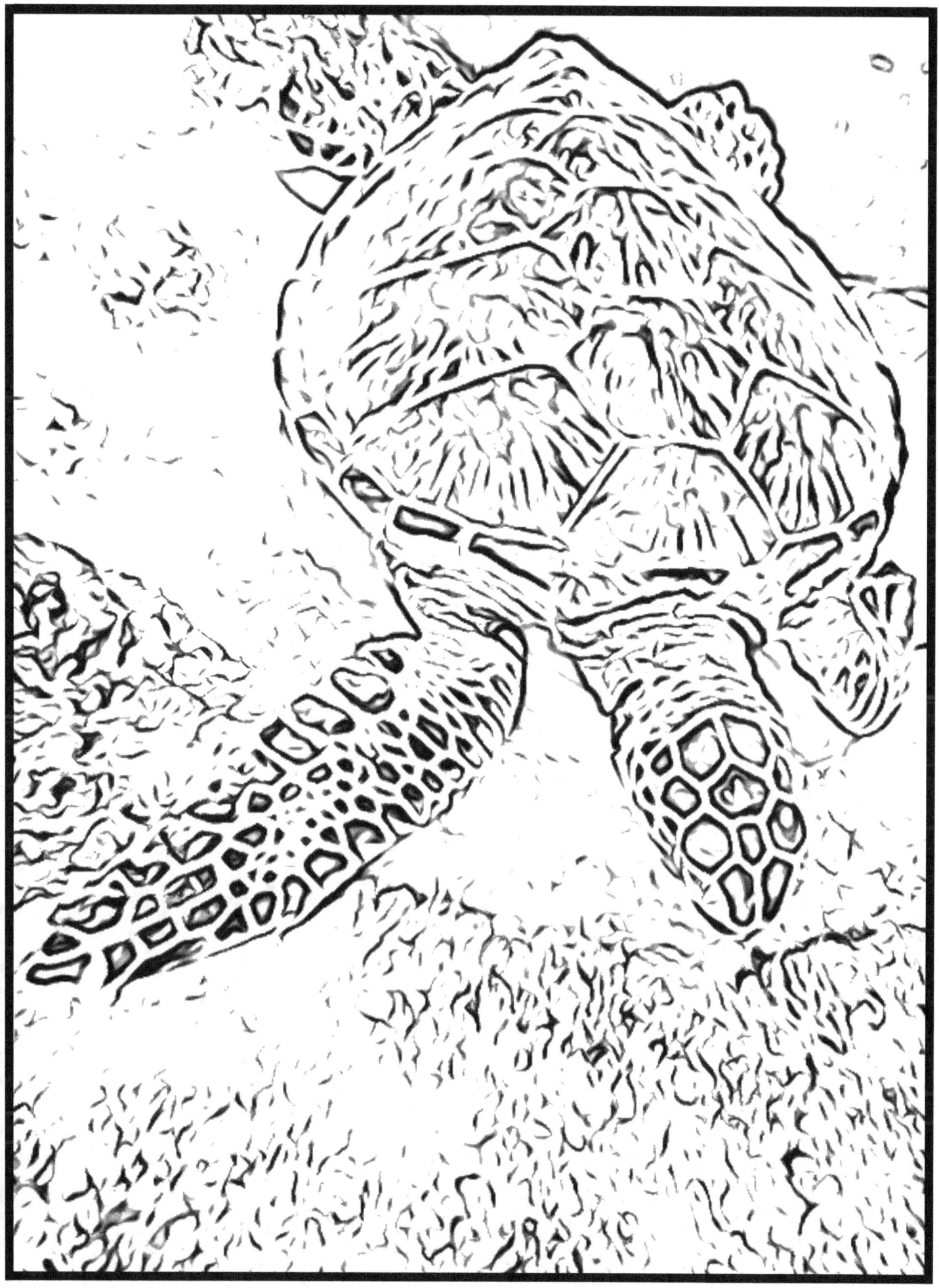

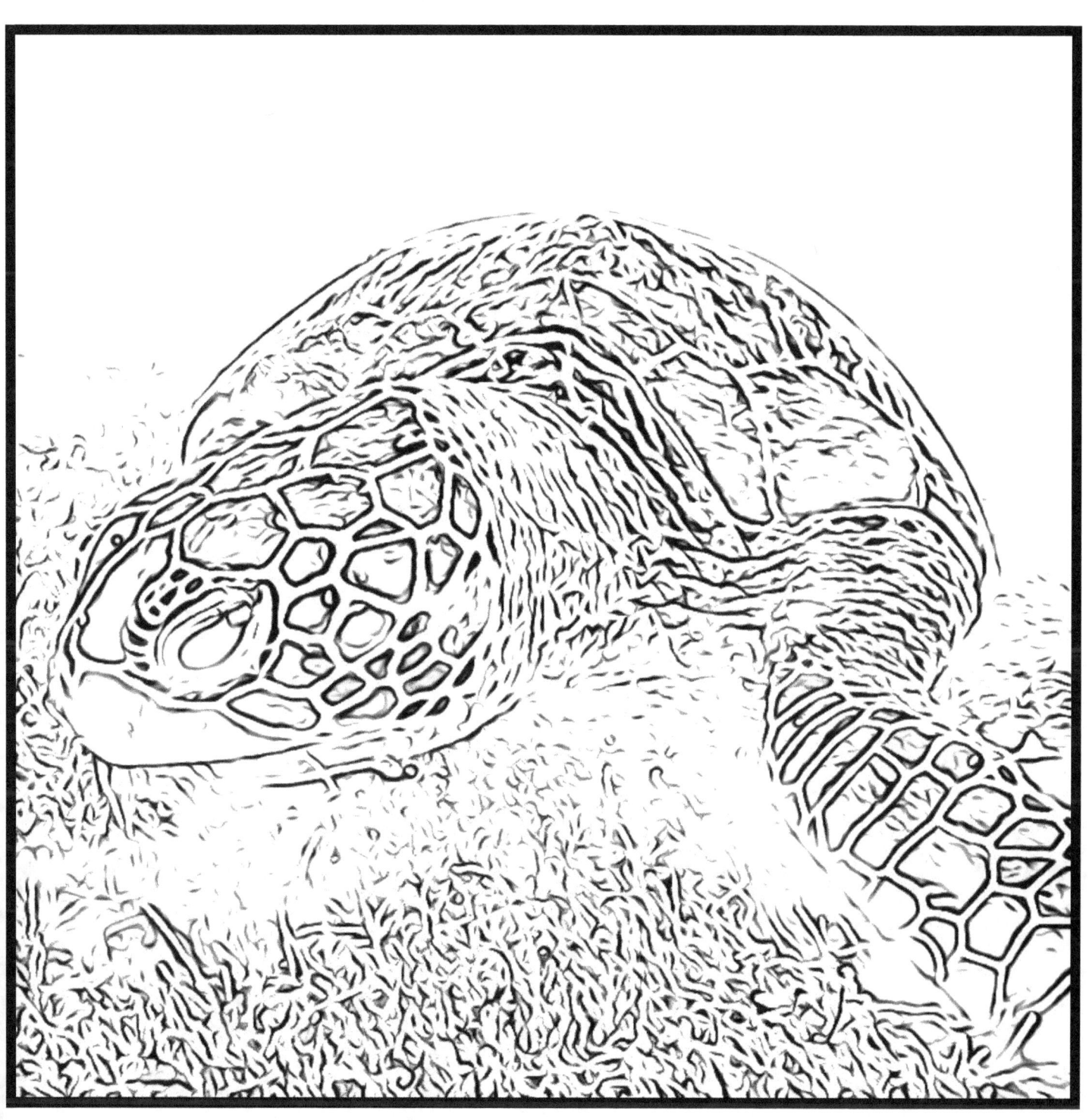

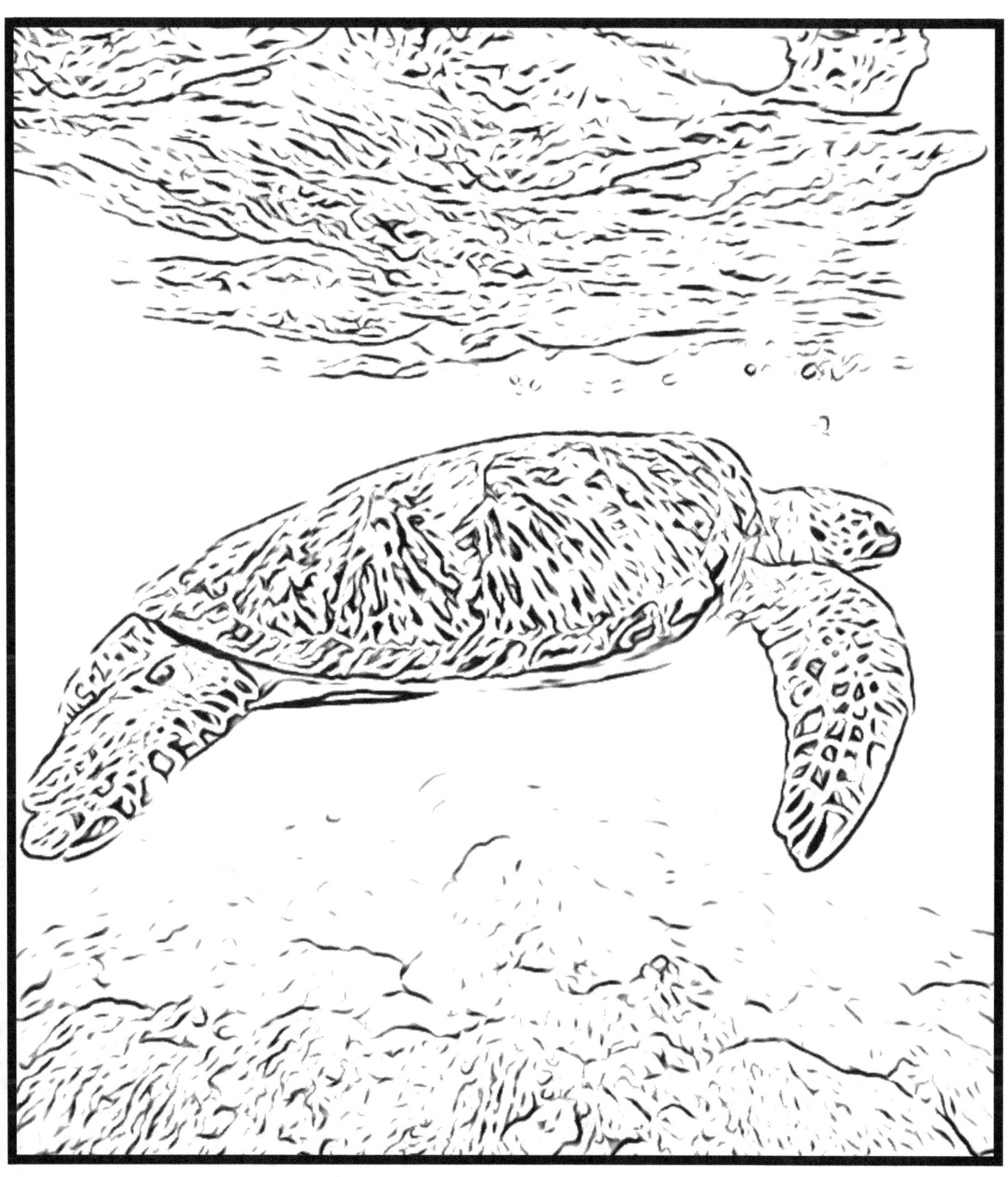

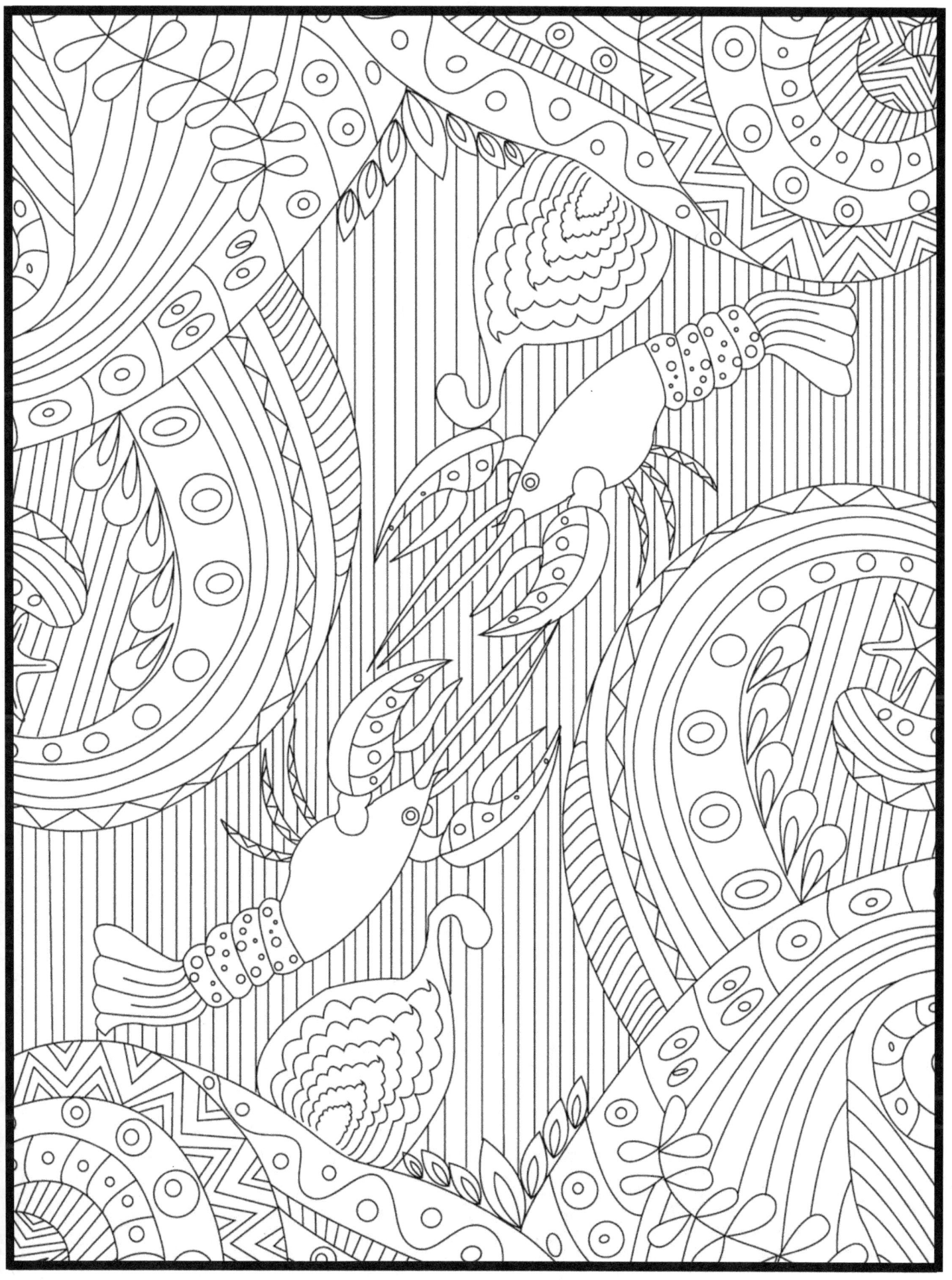

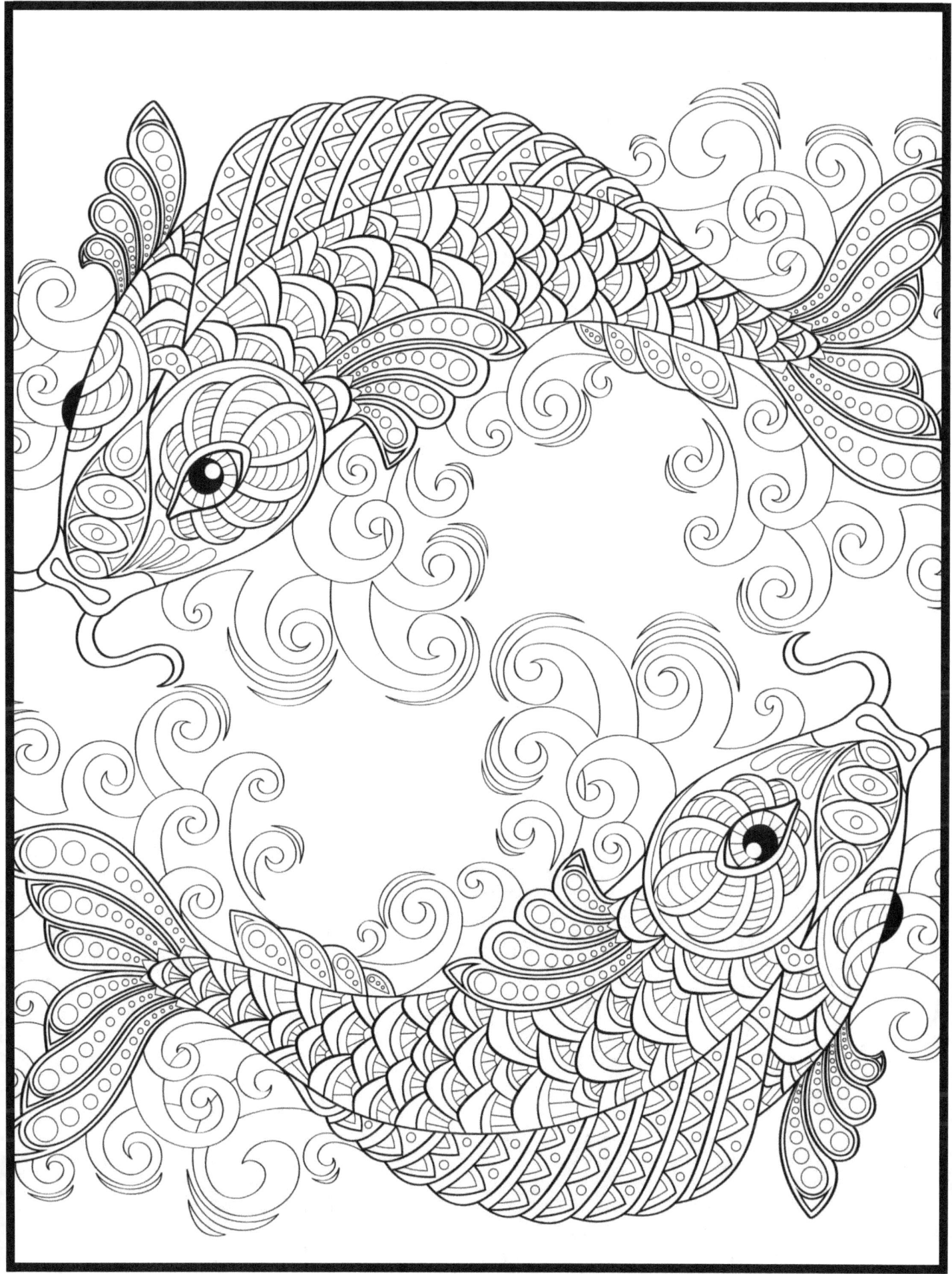

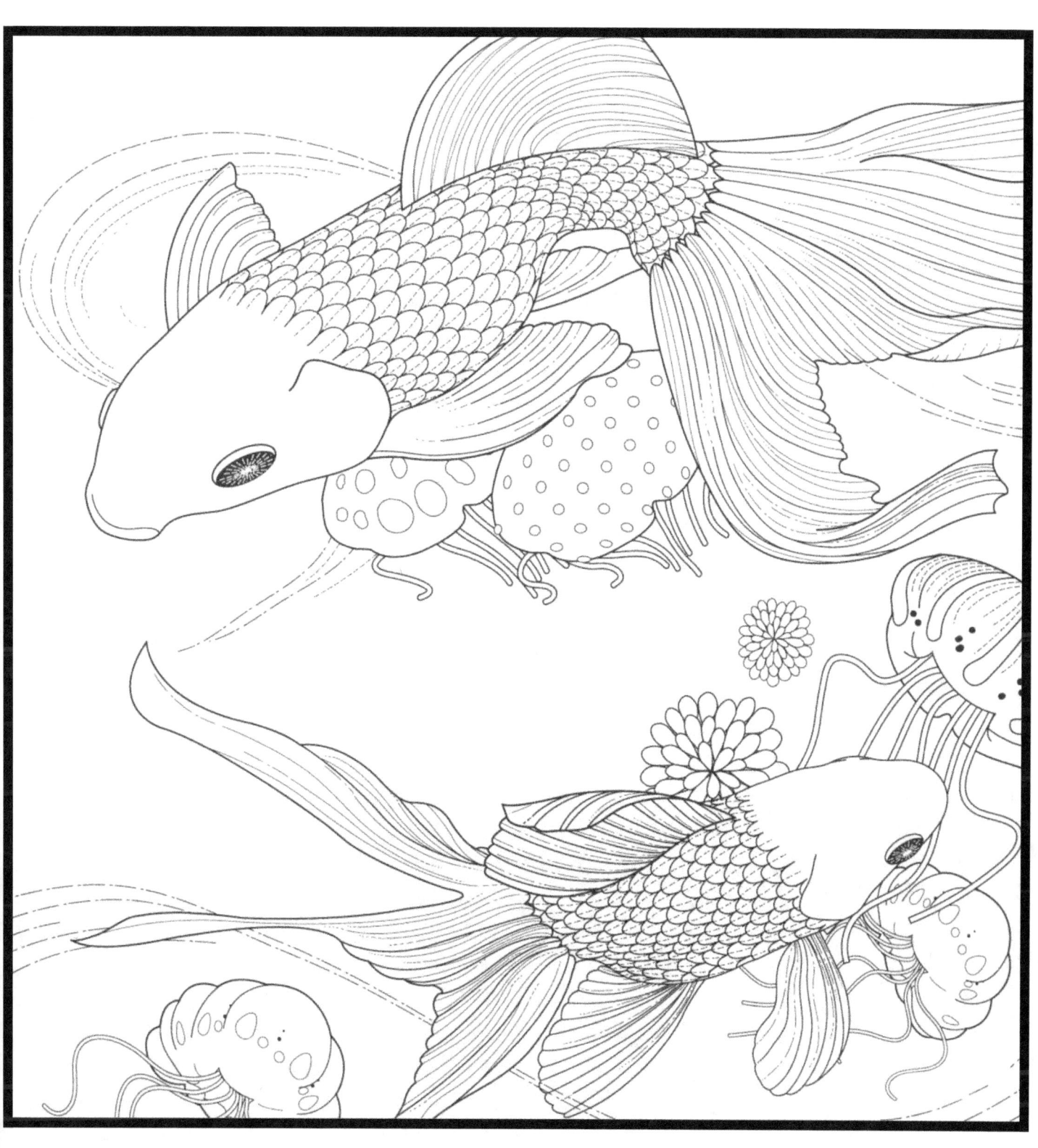

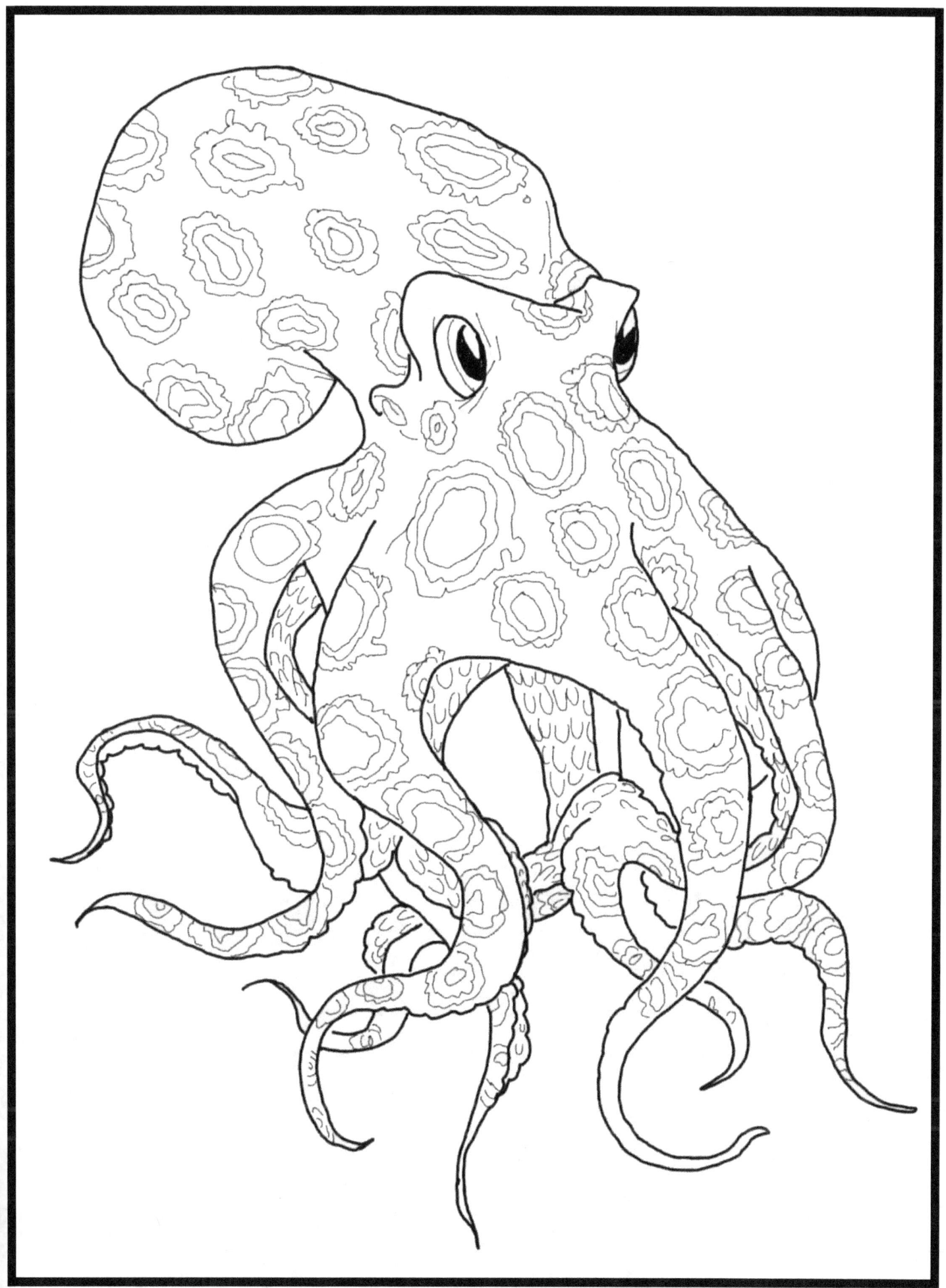

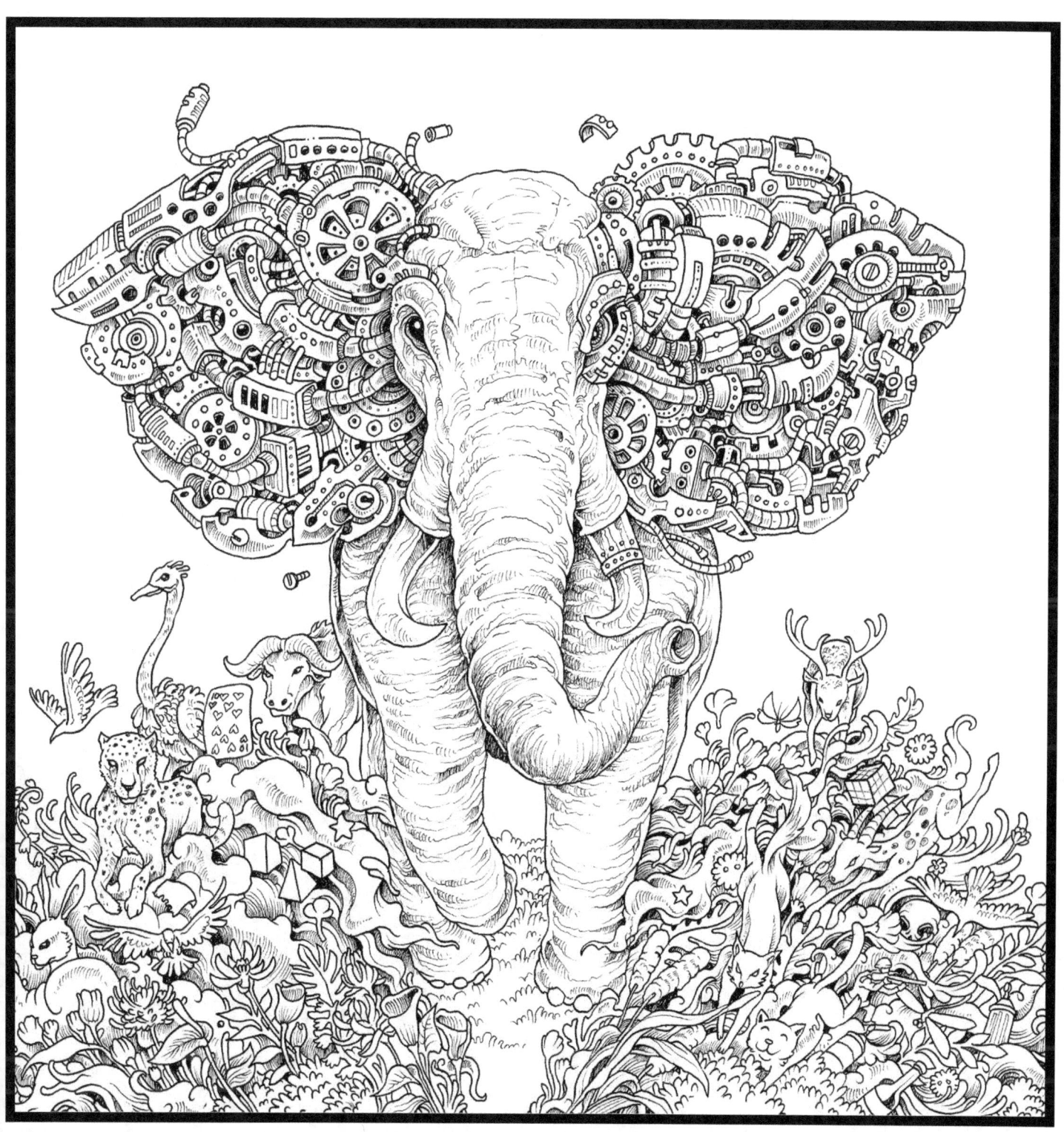

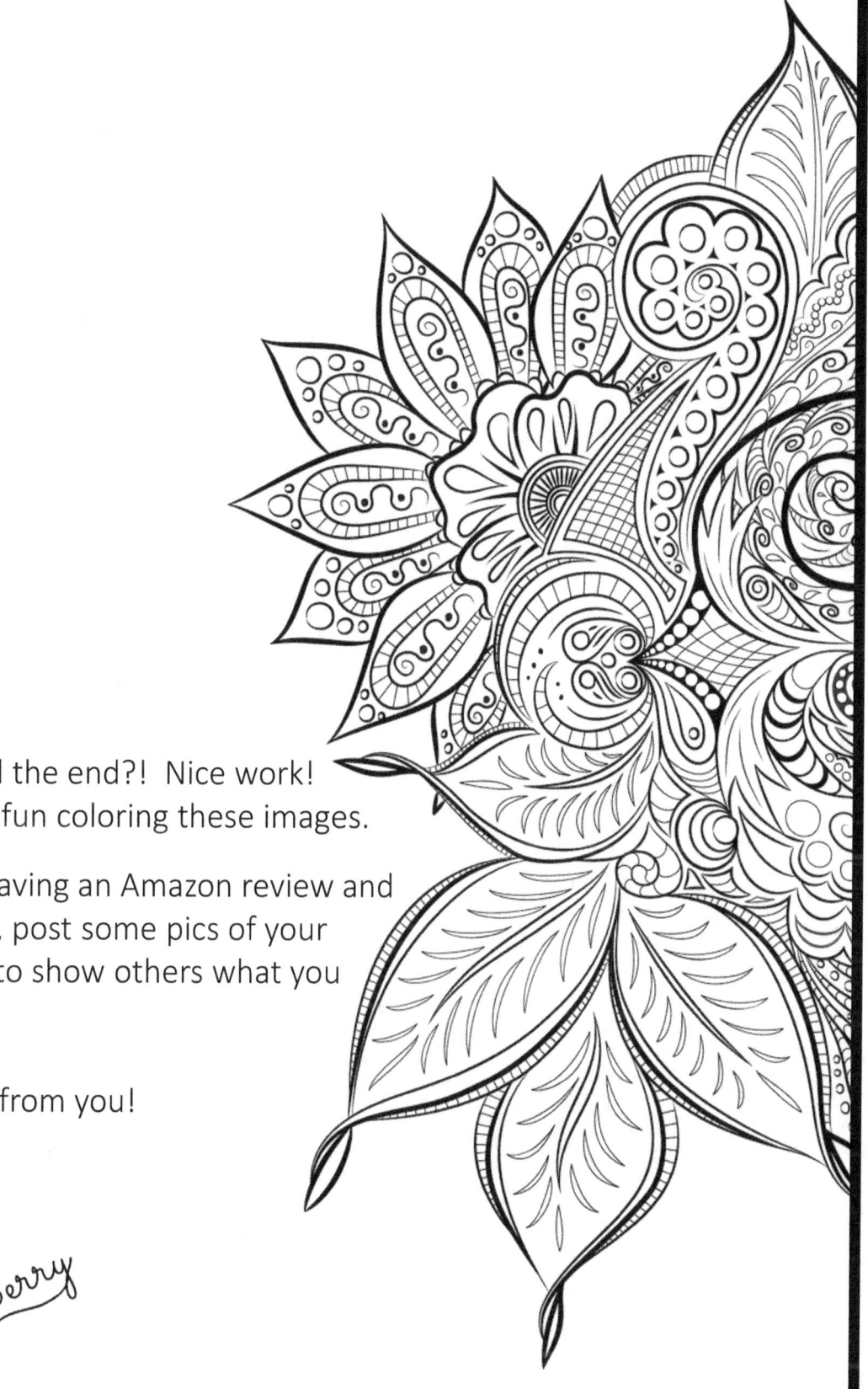

Wow, you reached the end?! Nice work!
We hope you had fun coloring these images.

Please consider leaving an Amazon review and if you are up for it, post some pics of your completed works to show others what you created!

We'd love to hear from you!

Stay Blessed

Luna Berry

www.ingramcontent.com/pod-product-compliance
Lightning Source LLC
Chambersburg PA
CBHW080941220526
45465CB00008BA/3115